Why the South Lost THE War

AND OTHER THINGS I DON'T UNDERSTAND

Other books by Bo Whaley:

All I Ever Wanted Was a Piece of Cornbread
    and a Cadillac
Bo Whaley's Field Guide to Southern Women
How to Love Yankees with a Clear Conscience
The Official Redneck Handbook
Redneckin' Made Easy
Rednecks and Other Bonafide Americans
The World Is Round But It's Crooked

Why the South Lost THE War

AND OTHER THINGS I DON'T UNDERSTAND

BO WHALEY

RUTLEDGE HILL PRESS
Nashville, Tennessee

To Doug, Ron, and Larry:

Doug for giving me a byline and
the opportunity to write my column;
Ron for signing me to a book contract;
and Larry for having the courage to publish them.

Published in Nashville, Tennessee, by Rutledge Hill Press, Inc.,
211 Seventh Avenue North, Nashville, Tennessee 37219

Typography by D&T/BAILEY, Nashville, Tennessee

Library of Congress Cataloging-in-Publication Data

Whaley, Bo, 1926–
    Why the south lost the war and other things I don't understand/
Bo Whaley.
        p. cm.
    ISBN 1-55853-161-0
    1. Southern States — Humor.   I. Title.
PN6231.S64W44   1992
814'.54 — dc20   92-5854
                                                                       CIP

2 3 4 5 6 7 — 97 96 95 94 93
Manufactured in the United States of America

CONTENTS

INTRODUCTION

It's a fact. Everything written must have a beginning and an ending. From the Bible to *Scarlett*, every book has these two characteristics. I've been writing for more than fifty years, fourteen for publication; but it took a little six-year-old girl in a first-grade class to impress upon me that "everything written must have a beginning." Never underestimate the wisdom of a six-year-old.

Several years ago, one of the primary schools in my hometown planned to emphasize writing during National Newspaper Week, and the school's principal invited me to speak to some sixty-five six-year-olds on the subject of newspaper publishing in general and writing in particular, especially newspaper columns and books.

I stood before the group on a Monday morning. The children were polite and as attentive as sixty-five six-year-olds can be. I spoke to them for about twenty-five minutes, saving the final five minutes for questions. I broke the ice with the first question, "What must any writer have before he can write anything?"

Little hands, some clean and some dirty, popped up. The answers were both interesting and varied.

"A typewriter!" yelled a little girl.

"Pencil and paper!" another called out.

"An eraser," said a little boy matter-of-factly with no visible sign of emotion.

All three were correct, and in my case the eraser especially. There were more—many more—but a pretty little brown-eyed girl sitting off to one side of the room knocked my hat in the creek when she said, "An idea."

Had I been assigning grades to the answers, she would have made an A-plus. I would have gotten at most a B-plus inasmuch as I was prepared to say "inspiration."

The little girl was absolutely right. Her answer is etched in

7

my mind and will remain there forever. To begin writing a book without an idea is like trying to start a car without gasoline, trying to eat without food, or trying to breathe without air. Any such attempt will prove futile. An author must take an idea and build upon it, not unlike a carpenter who lays a foundation before building a house or an artist who begins with his first stroke.

It follows that if an idea is basic to writing, inspiration runs a close second. Writing without inspiration is like kissing with your eyes open. You can get the job done, but the end result isn't very inspiring.

I am inspired to write because it affords me the opportunity to accomplish something few people are fortunate enough to enjoy in a lifetime: the opportunity to create. Good, bad, or indifferent, when I am finished with a manuscript or newspaper column, I have created something for posterity, something that has never been done before and will never be done again. And it is branded forever as mine. For some reason, that gives me a good feeling.

I was inspired to write this book because of a poem written by a nineteenth-century poet, Alfred Lord Tennyson, almost 150 years ago in 1854, "The Charge of the Light Brigade."

There are those familiar with my writing who will be amazed to learn that I read poetry. I do and have for many years. Like most writers, I dabble in it occasionally for my own pleasure.

Over the years I must have read "The Charge of the Light Brigade" at least fifty times, but as I read it almost a year ago it somehow took on an added significance, particularly the last five lines of the second stanza:

> Theirs not to make reply,
> Theirs not to reason why,
> Theirs but to do and die:
> Into the valley of Death
> Rode the six hundred.

These four lines hit me like a ton of bricks! I read them again and then read the entire poem again. I was hard-pressed to believe or understand what I had read or how the meaning of these five lines had somehow managed to escape me in previous readings. Being overly inquisitive and rarely ever taking things at face value, I wanted to know more. I went to the library and searched the shelves until I found what I needed. I wanted to read these lines in context. Here is what I found.

When at the Battle of Balaklava in 1854 the order was given for the charge into the valley where almost inescapable death awaited, the men of the Light Brigade responded at once, displaying the perfect discipline that had been fundamental to the British tradition. "Was there a man dismay'd?/Not tho' the soldier knew/Someone had blunder'd." (The second, third, and fourth lines of the second stanza). The soldier's place is never to argue against an order, never to hesitate obeying, or even to attempt to judge whether it is right or wrong.

Finished, I retreated and read the last five lines of the second stanza once again with particular attention to these three:

> Theirs not to make reply,
> Theirs not to reason why,
> Theirs but to do and die.

That's strong stuff, dedication. Actually, it's kamikaze, insane. I would never have made it in the Light Brigade. Having analyzed these three lines over and over, I always reach the same conclusion: I and my trusty steed would never have ridden into the valley of death. As I look at each line closely, here's why:

• "Theirs not to make reply." Had I been there, I would have had to make reply. No way would I have sat there mute while being told to go kill myself and probably my horse.

I would have spoken up. I ain't bashful, especially when my life is on the line, and I probably would have said something like, "Hey! Wait a cotton pickin' minute there, Big Al! I'm makin' reply whether I'm supposed to or not. What's this business 'bout ridin' off into the valley of Death? And didn' ya say a minute 'er two ago that somebody blundered? How 'bout tellin' us 'bout that. I mean, y'r words sound purty an' all that, but dadgummit man, it's me and these other fellas who's s'pose to ride off into some valley and probly not come back. I got a wife, two chillun, and some coon dogs back home. Whut 'bout them, Al? Heck man, let's talk this thing over f'r a spell befo' doin' anythin' dumb."

• "Theirs not to reason why." What's this? Not to reason why? You can bet the egg money I would reason why. Sounds to me like the whole plan originated at the funny farm. Had to be some government bureaucrat who came up with such a plan.

"I ain't no Phi Beta Kappa, Al, but even I know this is a dumb battle plan. You're a-talkin' 'bout us fightin' in some strange valley with both hands tied behind our backs. I ain't buyin' the plan, Al."

• "Theirs but to do and die." Man, that's permanent stuff he's talkin' 'bout. All cut and dried, ain't it? Do and die? I'd ruther talk about "don't and live."

"Looka heah, Al. Tell me some more 'bout this doin' and dyin'. You say our'n is but to do and die? Whut 'bout turnin' tail an' gittin' th' heck outta heah? I don' know 'bout the other 599, but as f'r me, I ain't los' nothin' in that valley. An' how 'bout you, Al? You plannin' on ridin' into th' valley, too, or is y'r plan to jus' stay heah and write 'bout it? I'd sorta like to know y'r feelins on this, Al."

Like I said, I take very little at face value, and had I been among the 600 back in 1854, I'd have had serious doubts and a whole bunch of questions. After hearing what Mr. Tennyson had to say about the probable future of the 600 men of the Light Brigade, there is little doubt in my mind. He would have had to use his eraser to change the last line of his second stanza to "Rode the five hundred and ninety-nine."

I didn't understand the logic when I first read it, and I don't understand it now. I do know that it inspired me to write this book because of so many things I don't understand, don't know, or was never told, like "Why the South lost *the* War." I just sorta have to come up with my own reasoning and explanations, and that's what I've done in this book.

Some things a fella don't learn in school or at home. Until I'm convinced otherwise, I'll just try and figure them out for myself and elaborate on them.

But I ain't narrow-minded. I'll listen. . . .

Why the South Lost THE War

AND OTHER THINGS I DON'T UNDERSTAND

SECTION ONE

THINGS I JUST DON'T UNDERSTAND

POLITICS EXPLAINED

ALGEBRA for FUN and PROFIT!

INSURANCE MADE SIMPLE

Figuring Out Women

HOW TO LOVE YANKEES WITH A CLEAR CONSCIENCE

2000 YEARS OF POLITICAL WISDOM LARGE TYPE EDITION

LAWYERS, SHARKS, and other PREDATORS

HOW COME DOCTORS TALK LIKE THAT. you, too, can sound like a REAL DOCTOR!

WHY THE SOUTH LOST *THE* WAR

Having lived for four years as a boy just nine miles from Andersonville National Cemetery in Andersonville, Georgia, I heard a lot as a youngster about *the* war. Northerners referred to it as the Civil War; Southerners as the War Between the States. Hard-core Dixie loyalists who will never give up called it the War of Yankee Aggression as well as the War for Southern Independence.

While I've never argued the pros and cons of either name for the war, many on both sides of the Mason–Dixon line still do. Though generations removed from Fort Sumter and Gettysburg, a wrong word can get a fella in a bunch of trouble.

The one thing that has troubled me through the years is why the South lost. Just ask the question, and you will get an answer—on both sides of the Mason–Dixon Line. The only thing I know for sure is that when it was all over, the North had put one in the *W* column, and the South began clean-up operations.

I am not a scholar of *the* war. I studied about it when I had to and listened to war stories told to me by my grandfather, Wes Whaley, who no doubt heard them from his father, Russell Whaley, who may have been there. I don't know. I wasn't. Neither was my grandfather.

I may well be the only living soul in Georgia never to have seen *Gone With the Wind*, and I have no plans to go see it until some theater runs it backwards and it comes out right. I've read the book several times, but I honestly have never seen the movie. Is that a crime in Georgia, especially living just two hours from Tara? If it is, I plead guilty.

I really don't know why the South lost *the* war, but I have some thoughts on it. I can't document them, but in my mind they make sense—three in particular:

• There is the theory long held by many, particularly in North Georgia, that the reason the South lost *the* war was because of a breakdown in communications between Union and Confederate soldiers.

In early September 1864, the armies were going at it tooth and nail on the outskirts of Atlanta. The Confederates had gained the upper hand and were on the verge of annihilating the Union forces near Stone Mountain when two Union soldiers appeared on top of the mountain. One began shouting down to the Confederate boys, "We surrender! We surrender!"

"What'd they say, Luke?" Corporal Bobby Joe asked.

"Danged if'n I know, Bobby Joe," Luke answered. "I can't understand a word they're asayin', can you?"

"Nope, not a dang word."

Again from the top of the mountain, "We surrender!"

"Whadda ya think, Luke?"

"Gotta be some sorta Yankee trick, Bobby Joe."

"Tha's what I think. Let 'em have it!"

Who knows? Maybe the South would have won *the* war right then and there if either Luke or Bobby Joe could have understood what the Yankees were saying.

• Another popular theory, especially in and around South Georgia, is that the Confederate forces experienced a food shortage during fierce fighting north of Savannah in October 1864 and were forced to surrender. My grandpa told me about it.

"Well, it was like this, son. We was really gettin' the best of 'em until one night when a squad of them Union soldiers somehow slipped behind our lines and swapped food wagons. They took a wagon load of grits and left in its place a wagon load of cream of wheat. Two days later, we had to surrender, and General Robert ('Bubba') Treadwell later explained why. He said that there just won't no way that his southern boys could fight on Yankee grits. They just plumb give out, he said."

• I have my own theory, and that is that the demise of Dixie actually took place in a coffee shop north of Atlanta in the little town of Acworth. I think this is what happened in November 1864.

Southern hospitality is well known, and that's what did the South in and caused it to lose *the* war. A stranger came into the coffee shop, sat down, and ordered a cup of coffee. It was a cold and blustery night, and in the booth next to the stranger sat Charley Mack and his girlfriend, Mary Sue. They had been to a square dance in Calhoun and had stopped in for a late-night snack.

Charley Mack struck up a conversation with the stranger that went like this:

"Howdy! Been travelin' some?" asked Charley Mack.

"Right, a little," the stranger answered.

"You fum roun' heah?"

"No. Just passing through."

"I see. My name's Charley Mack Burnley, and this here's my girlfriend, Mary Sue," Charley Mack said, extending his hand. Mary Sue smiled.

"Glad to know you. I'm Billy," the stranger said.

"Pleased to meetcha," said Mary Sue, also extending her hand.

"Thank you."

For the better part of an hour, the stranger and Charley Mack, with an occasional smile from Mary Sue, talked. Then, the stranger rose to leave, reached in his pocket, and pulled out some change.

"I'll gitcha coffee," Charley Mack volunteered.

"Thanks, thanks very much. That's nice of you," the stranger said.

"Where 'bouts ya headed?" Charley Mack asked.

"Going to the beach—Savannah."

"It's nice down there this time o' year," Mary Sue said.

"Goin' by y'sef?" asked Charley Mack.

"No. Oh, no. Some friends are joining me just south of Atlanta later."

"Well, have a good trip, an' if ya git back this way an' I kin do anythin' f'r ya', just holler," Charley Mack told him.

"Thank you, I'll do that," said the stranger, shaking hands with Charley Mack and tipping his blue hat to Mary Sue. "Oh, by the way. Would you by any chance have a match? I . . ."

"Shoot, I reckon! Here, take these," Charley Mack said, handing him a small box. "Jus' keep 'em. I got more out in my wagon."

"Thank you. Well, I'll be on my way. Have a trail to blaze," the stranger said.

"See ya. By th' way, whut's y'r las' name, Billy?"

"Sherman. William T.," the stranger said. "But you can just call me Billy. Good-bye!"

Charley Mack and Mary Sue looked at each other and smiled.

"Nice fella that Billy Sherman, ain't he Mary Sue?"

"Shore is . . . rail nice, Charley Mack."

And that is why I think the South lost *the* war. Southern hospitality and a small box of matches extended to a stranger named Billy Sherman, William T., to be exact.

A FEW THINGS I DON'T UNDERSTAND

I'm ready to concede that I really don't know very much. I once thought I knew a little bit about a lot of things, but no more.

It seems that the more I contemplate life around me, the less I know about it. There are just so many things I don't understand. Like . . .

- I don't understand blood pressure readings. What does it *really* mean if it's 130/80? Is that the time to call in the family and a priest or a preacher, or is it merely the odds on the Notre Dame–Penn State game? Nobody has ever explained blood pressure readings to me, although my blood pressure has been taken repeatedly for years.

- I don't understand the metric system. And furthermore, I don't give a hoot about it. I don't really care to have some sportscaster tell me that the slotback ran eighty-five meters for a touchdown or that my favorite stock car driver is in the sixty-sixth lap of a 500 kilometer race.

- I don't understand what Celsius means. I do under- stand that when—in mid-August—I hear a weatherper- son say that the temperature is 104 degrees, I momentarily suffocate until I hear that it is 72 degrees Celsius. I'm com- fortable with 40 degrees in January until some spoilsport meteorologist follows with ". . . but it's 8 degrees Cel- sius." I'll take Celsius in August and Fahrenheit in Jan- uary, thank you.

- I don't understand what you do with math after grad- uation, unless you go on to teach it to others who won't understand what to do with it after graduation either. I can truthfully say that since I graduated from high school, not one person has ap- proached me on the street and asked, "Excuse me, sir, but could you tell me the value of X or Y?" And postulates and axioms? Forget 'em. As best I can recall from having worked for years in Michigan on the Canadian border, postulates are ladies of the evening who sneak across the border after dark to entertain men for a fee . . . if the men approach them and axiom.

• I don't understand ice hockey or what particular significance the blue line has. And what the heck is "icing"? Down here in Dixie it has always had to do with cake making, the final touch so to speak.

• I don't understand what "proof" means to a bottle of whiskey or "octane" to a gallon of gasoline. But I think I do understand that it would be disastrous if the whiskey distilleries and the oil refineries somehow got them mixed up, resulting in my automobile weaving from one side of the highway to the other and a blue flame emitting from my mouth after having downed a Scotch and water and lit up a cigarette.

• I don't understand how, after all these years, I still can't make syrup and biscuits come out even. There's always a little of one remaining after the other runs out. For anyone who is a native of anyplace north of Richmond

(and therefore not educated in the fine art of "sopping"), disregard the foregoing and concentrate your thoughts on the blue line and "icing." But should you have an insatiable desire to learn, remember that proper sopping etiquette dictates that you sop from left to right, making gentle and rhythmic swipes around your plate and through the sugar cane—*always* sugar cane—syrup with a cathead biscuit. Anybody who would dare to sop maple syrup would eat cream of wheat. *Cathead* biscuits? That's another ballgame entirely and too delicate to get into at this juncture. I will tell you that cathead biscuits are the best biscuits in the world, especially if cooked in a woodstove. Trust me.

• I don't understand why anyone would want to live north of Nashville. I'm convinced that God has a mansion in the Belle Meade section of the Music City and embraces country music.

• I don't understand where clouds go.

• I don't understand why all of a sudden America is about out of pennies. Does Oliver North have them all stashed in that little metal box on the floor of his clothes closet into which he said he dropped all his change at night and came up with $15,000? At least that's where he said it came from.

• I don't understand how anybody could like Jane Fonda or dislike her daddy.

• I don't understand how instant replays work. A guy runs ninety-two yards for a touchdown, and before I can flip my Bic, danged if he don't do it again. I saw the same fella score four times in twelve seconds on successive fifty-four-yard runs during a recent telecast, but the score remained 6–0. How could that happen? Four times six is still twenty-four, ain't it?

• I don't understand how Jesse Jackson makes a living.

• I don't understand what the U.N. does, but I know who pays for whatever it is it does.

• I don't understand automobile sticker prices. Has anybody *ever* paid the sticker price for a car?

• I don't understand what "last" has to do with my shoe size. Why not "first?"

• I don't understand how spies know when they've run out of invisible ink. I mean, a spy could write a fifty-page espionage report, have the last twenty-seven pages come out blank, and get his tail shipped off to Siberia in winter . . . and never really know why.

• I don't understand what sort of container Styrofoam is shipped in.

• I don't understand why Ybor City, Florida, is pronounced "Ebo City" or why Thibodeaux, Louisiana, is pronounced "Tippydoe."

• I don't understand how a kaleidoscope works or how broken glass can make such pretty pictures.

• I don't understand how Ralph Nader makes a living.

• I don't understand Reaganomics and never have. Of course, I never understood Carternomics, Fordonomics, Nixonomics, Johnsonomics, or Kennedynomics either. The best I have been able to figure out is that you just send all you can to Washington and hope to get a little in return.

• I don't understand why we drive on parkways and park in driveways. Try explaining that to someone who just arrived from Haiti.

• I don't understand why store prices are never even money. Why not an even $2.00 for crackers, $1.25 for peanut butter, and $15,000 for a new car? Why $1.99, $1.19, $14,999?

• I don't understand why

cats bathe so much. They don't do a heck of a lot to get dirty just sitting around on the backs of sofas and automobile hoods with their motor running, staring at you like they know what you're thinking. I don't own a cat. I've never owned one. I don't want nothin' in my house that bathes more than I do, eats rats, and thinks like a psychiatrist.

• I don't understand why cars are engineered to go 120 when the speed limit is 55 or 65. Just asking for trouble, I think.

• I don't understand how cruise control works. And what if it gets stuck on eighty-five in the mountains of Tennessee? I guess that's when you really find out what those "runaway truck" ramps are for.

• I don't understand how a microwave oven gets the soup hot enough to take the hide off a hog without heating the bowl.

• I don't understand how a convicted murderer can be sentenced to life imprisonment plus forty years in 1984 and be back out on the street in 1991.

• I don't understand what *habeas corpus* is, or a *corpus delicti*, but both sound morbid. I just know that I don't want to own or be either.

• I don't understand why some people drink hot tea when they have a refrigerator full of ice.

• I don't understand disco dancing or how it ever got started. Did some guy and gal drop concrete blocks on their toes?

• I don't understand banks, but I do understand that the person who does the commercials ain't the one who makes the loans.

• I don't understand which is the opposite sex.

• I don't understand what holds up a strapless evening gown. I *think* I do, but I've always been afraid to ask.

• I don't understand where seedless oranges and grapes come from.

• I don't understand why telephone information operators are always in such a hurry. Don't they have to stay until the end of their eight-hour shifts?

• I don't understand why, if we are going to have No Smoking sections, we can't have No Jukebox and No Cheap Perfume sections.

• I don't understand why a church will build a new sanctuary to seat only 600 when it has a membership of 1,185.

● And finally, I don't understand why we don't pray more when we don't need anything and everything's running along smoothly. You know, just to say, "Thank you, Lord. I appreciate all you've done for me."

No, sir. I just don't understand why I don't understand.

MORE THINGS I DON'T UNDERSTAND

Will Rogers once said, "We are all ignorant, only on different subjects." The more I think about it, the more I realize that Will Rogers was right, especially in my case.

I already listed some things I don't understand. Here's an update, more things I don't understand:

- I don't understand why some men wear both a belt and suspenders, unless they subscribe to the theory "better safe than sorry."
- I don't understand divestiture or telephone bills. But then, does anybody? And who gets my money? Looks to me like it is divided about ten ways so that everybody gets a slice of the divestiture pie.
- I don't understand what a doctor means when he walks into the examining room and tells you to "strip to the waist." Do you remove your shirt or pants? Remove either and you've complied, right?
- I don't understand why possums keep trying to cross the road after seeing what happened to their predecessors when they tried.
- I don't understand why ants never take a break or demand overtime pay.
- I don't understand why glove compartments are so named when most of them have everything but gloves in them.
- I don't understand why shoelaces never break until you're running five minutes late for work.
- I don't understand what the STP stands for on a can of oil treatment.
- I don't understand why some 7–Eleven stores stay open twenty-four hours a day. If they insist on doing it, shouldn't they be renamed twenty-four-hour stores?
- I don't understand VCRs, but I don't concern myself with it. Most people don't understand VCRs.
- I don't understand people who say, "I just don't have the time." Don't we all have the same amount, twenty-four hours a day?

- I don't understand the meaning of "safety" matches. Any match capable of burning a building to the ground or destroying thousands of acres of timberland doesn't sound very safe to me.
- I don't understand people who take up two parking spaces with one car.
- I don't understand why most public restrooms have hot-air hand dryers instead of paper towels. My hands always get dry before the thing stops blowing. Not being a wasteful person, I just stand there with my dry hands under it until it stops. Actually, I'd rather use my shirttail— and have.
- I don't understand it when I hear somebody yell, "Sit down in front!" When God made us, he never intended that we sit down in front. In the first place, it is an impossible feat to accomplish. In the second place, try it and you'll dang near break your back.
- I don't understand why, when giving a speech, I'm always introduced by someone I've never met.
- I don't understand why, when I do my laundry, I always come up one sock short. There must be thousands of bureau drawers containing thousands of mismatched socks.
- I don't understand where the fat goes when somebody loses thirty pounds on a diet.
- I don't understand how a brown cow can eat green grass and give white milk and yellow butter.
- I don't understand how a 67,000-ton passenger ship keeps from sinking.
- I don't understand why nothing "tears along the dotted line."
- I don't understand why the sole of my left shoe always gets a hole in it before the sole of my right one. Don't they take the same number of steps?
- I don't understand why, during the course of a year, I receive hundreds of letters with the announcement in bold print on the outside of the envelope, "You may have won a million dollars!" or "Congratulations! You are a sweepstakes winner," but I never receive anything.
- I don't understand how I can spill an eight-ounce glass of iced tea and have two gallons drench the tablecloth.
- I don't understand why, when I drop a coin or a cuff link, it seeks refuge in the darkest corner of the room or

underneath the bed.

- I don't understand why zippers always get stuck in the "down" position.
- I don't understand how fishing lines, garden hoses, extension cords, paper clips, and wire coat-hangers can become so tangled and twisted when nobody's touched them.
- I don't understand why coin machines never malfunction when you have a pocketful of change, but invariably will if you possess but two quarters and there's no place nearby to get change for a dollar.
- I don't understand what hermits do with their spare time.
- I don't understand why the one book I need from the library is always checked out.
- I don't understand why blisters always appear on the fingers we use most.
- I don't understand why, when I sneeze, folks up North immediately say, "Gesundheit!" In the South

they always say "Bless you!" And it's always the same, no matter how many successive sneezes I manage.

- I don't understand why it is that when a batter is being intentionally walked by a pitcher, the pitcher still delivers the four required pitches, way outside, before the batter can move along to first base with a base on balls. Why not just tell the umpire to move him along and bring on the next batter?
- I don't understand why men's coat buttons are on the right side but women's are on the left. There has to be an explanation, but I have no idea what it is. Just another example of something I never learned in school or wasn't paying attention to when it was being discussed.

And if it will serve as any consolation to you, let me assure you that you aren't the only one who doesn't understand what's going on in the Middle East.

A FEW THINGS I DON'T KNOW

Fact is fact, and it's a fact that there are some things that I just don't know. My lack of knowledge surfaces primarily when driving on America's interstate highways, usually in Dixieland.

Other than listening to zillions of radio talk shows, there is little else to do other than dodge flattened possums and beer cans, or maybe catch an occasional tourist from New Jersey changing a flat tire.

Radio talk shows keep me awake, trying to anticipate the next stupid question and the next stupid answer. Psychologist hosts are the worst, the bottom of the talk-show barrel. They know everything, from how to burp a baby to how to get squirrels out of the attic. Put a psychologist on the radio, and it makes my forefinger twitch wanting to stop at the next pay phone and call in. Psychologists become experts when the microphone is turned on.

While I've never called a radio talk show, here are some of the questions I would pose if I did call. I know the answers would be forthcoming:

- What's the difference between beer and ale?
- What is *perestroika* as opposed to *glasnost?*
- What's the difference between a traverse and a petit jury?
- What's the difference between a speedometer and an odometer?
- What do barometric readings mean?
- What exactly is ground clutter?
- What's the difference between nylon, rayon, and Dacron?
- Where is polyester raised? And how is it harvested?
- What's the difference between a first cousin and a second cousin once removed? And how does one come up with a double first cousin?
- What's the difference between a bagel, a bugle, and a bungle?

- Does a falling tree make noise if there's no one within a hundred miles to hear it?
- What does AM stand for in radio parlance? Or FM?
- What does WD stand for in WD-40? Is there a WD-30? Or WD-50? If so, is WD-30 less expensive? Is WD-50 more expensive?
- What's the difference between an abridged and an unabridged dictionary?
- What does the term *bare facts* mean to a nudist?
- What's the difference between fluorescent, incandescent, and irridescent lighting? Any similarity to adolescent?
- I know about dry-cell batteries. Are there any wet-cell batteries?
- When does a kitten become a cat? Or a puppy a dog?
- Where is the Left Bank? Is it opposite the Right Bank?
- What is the Gaza Strip? Is it a dance of some sort? Or maybe a race track?
- What size shoe does Big Foot wear?
- Does the Loch Ness monster throw a Halloween party?
- How deep is a fathom?
- How long is a furlong?
- Can you "back up and go ahead"?
- Is it possible for one to actually be "beside himself"?
- Do owls ever have cataracts?

I really don't know the answers. Maybe you do.

WHERE HAVE THE OLD TRADITIONS GONE?

With many of us in the over-fifty group, traditions have either disappeared or are in the process of doing so. Here are some that I grew up with. They're gone, and I miss 'em. How many are—or were—familiar to you?

- Boys shooting marbles
- An old man whittling
- An old lady churning
- A child riding a stick-horse
- A tire swing
- Rain on a tin roof
- A service station attendant removing a whisk broom from his back pocket, sweeping your floorboard, washing your windows, checking your tires, and then asking, "Wammee to check y'r oil?"
- Pouring peanuts into a bottle of Coke
- Rabbit tobacco
- A pocket watch
- Brilliantine
- Hula-hoops
- Davy Crockett coonskin caps
- A homemade scooter
- A game of cowboys and Indians
- A new house with a front porch
- A feather bed
- Linoleum floors
- A girl blushing
- A band without a sound system big enough to fill three freight cars
- A spotlight on an automobile
- A girl wearing loose-fitting jeans
- Boys naked as a hammer handle swimming in a creek
- Making homemade candy
- A tuning fork
- Licking the chocolate out of the bowl
- Rolling a cigarette
- A kid catching a June bug or a lightning bug
- Stealing a watermelon
- A washboard or a wash pot

And more . . .
- A nonfilter cigarette
- A mule and plow
- A real hobo

- A fountain pen that uses real ink
- A pair of brogans
- A case of sore eyes
- Rat cheese (or hoop cheese)
- Black automobile tires
- A prom party
- Knickers
- A rolling store
- Anybody paying cash for a motel or hotel room
- A mule and wagon
- A bologna sandwich
- An ice or milk truck making home deliveries
- A doctor making a house call
- A movie you would take your mother to see
- Men pitching pennies to a crack on the sidewalk
- Black-and-white wingtip shoes
- A checkers game being played with bottle caps in front of a country store
- A T-shirt with nothing printed on it
- A car without a radio
- Anybody chopping stove wood
- A family just sitting around talking to one another
- A *real* milkshake like drugstores used to make
- A sign in front of a filling station, We Fix Flats
- Pants that button up
- Manual typewriters
- A girl's bathing suit that would pass Grandma's inspection
- Good news on the front page
- A Saturday afternoon shoot-em-up movie
- A game of leapfrog
- A Jew's harp
- Rubber guns
- Hadacol
- A mustard plaster
- Stick (kitchen) matches

And the saddest of all, Cokes in six-ounce bottles are all but extinct.
Shame . . .

I NEED ANSWERS

I don't usually squander my time on questions of a trivial nature, but the time has come for the answers to questions of utmost importance. I do dabble in trivia, and with a world-renowned and recognized expert on the subject—Ludlow Porch, longtime congenial talk-show host on Atlanta radio station WSB-AM. I am no match for Ludlow. But then, neither are most other trivia buffs.

The world is waiting for answers to these questions. Can you help?

- Who winds the watch used on CBS's "60 Minutes"?
- Where does Webster look when *he* needs a definition?
- Whatever happened to the nine-digit ZIP Code?
- Did Robin Hood and Jesse James have bank accounts?
- Who hears the Pope's confession?
- Who edits what the editor writes?
- Whatever happened to Alice Lon? Did she get tangled up in all her petticoats and strangle?
- What was Daisy Mae's last name?
- Does Perry Como take Nytol?
- What kind of pipe tobacco did Bing Crosby smoke? And did he ever sing in the shower?
- What do you give a giraffe for a sore throat?
- How many miles per gallon does Richard Petty get?
- What was the name of "The Boston Strangler"? Or "The Fiddler on the Roof"? Or "The Phantom of the Opera"?
- What was the name of Tim McCoy's horse?
- What size shoe does Tiny Tim wear?
- When Dolly Parton has a chest cold, does she hurt more than other women?
- Who was Arthur Godfrey's announcer?
- Who killed John Wilkes Booth?
- Do Christine Jorgensen and Renee Richards go to the men's or women's restroom?

- How deep was the Black Hole of Calcutta?
- How many degrees are there in "The Bermuda Triangle"?
- What is the capital of Afghanistan?
- What was the final score of the baseball game in which the "mighty" Casey struck out?
- Whatever happened to the 52–60 club?
- What was the name of the last country song the late great Hank Williams recorded? (This is the only answer I know: "I'll Never Get Out Of This World Alive.")
- What is Little Richard's last name?
- Does Fabian have another name? Is Fabian his first or last name?
- What was the name of Eleanor Roosevelt's newspaper column?
- Did Wimpy, of "Popeye" fame, eat onions on his hamburgers?
- Who was Roy Rogers's first wife?
- What is the brand name of James Bond's (007) cigarette lighter?
- What was the name of Sad Sack's girlfriend in World War II?
- Who was the owner of the boardinghouse in "Gunsmoke"?
- What is Aunt Jemima's real name?
- What was the name of Tom Sawyer's girlfriend? Did Huckleberry Finn have one?
- Whatever happened to Edgar Bergen's dummies— Charlie McCarthy, Mortimer Snerd, Effie Clinker, and Podine Buffington?
- What was the name of the theme song of "The Green Hornet"?
- What was "Smilin' Jack's" last name? What kind of airplane did he fly?
- Who were the seven original astronauts?
- Of the Seven Dwarfs, which one was the only one to wear glasses?
- What was the street address of Fibber McGee and Molly?
- Did the Lone Ranger have any brothers or sisters? What was his real name?
- What caliber pistol did Wyatt Earp carry?
- What was "Gorgeous" George's real name? What perfume did he use to spray the wrestling ring before he would enter it?

These are but a few of the questions the world is waiting to have answered. Any help would be appreciated.

SOME SITUATIONS CONFUSE ME

If you've made it this far, you may have concluded that I live in a constant state of confusion and misunderstanding, comprehending little or nothing. Not true. I do live in a constant state of observation, watching with interest everything that goes on around me and writing about much of it.

Some of my favorite haunts for people-watching are airports, hotel lobbies, sporting events, and restaurants—especially restaurants.

In making my rounds, I tend to get involved in ticklish situations. In most cases I find myself at a loss as to what to do at the time. A prime example happened in a very nice restaurant in a very nice resort hotel in North Carolina. How nice is North Carolina? Well, I've been spending my vacations there since I was a boy. That's a long time.

I was having breakfast. The dining room was quite crowded, including a tour group of about twenty-five people from Connecticut. To get the group's attention, the tour leader tapped repeatedly on his water glass with his knife, then climbed up on his chair. He gained their attention all right, but not so much by the repeated rapping on his water glass but more because of something he neglected to do in his haste to get dressed earlier. Possibly he overslept.

I had a ringside seat. In his haste, the tour leader had neglected to (1) fasten a very inconspicuous button on his shirt in the abdominal area and (2) zip up a very conspicuous zipper on his trousers.

There I sat, an outsider, listening to his announcements regarding the day's schedule of events between giggles and snickers from some members of the group he was addressing from his lofty perch. Not one person volunteered to approach him with the information he desperately needed to know or slip him a note containing the pertinent facts.

What would you have done had you been sitting in my chair? Would you have:

- Continued eating and tried to ignore the obvious?
- Joined the giggling and laughter?
- Left a delicious breakfast and walked away?

I did none of the above. What I did do was to scribble a short but informative note on a napkin and then requested the restaurant manager somehow to slip it to the guy discreetly, if indeed that was possible to do with a man flaunting an errant zipper standing on a chair in full view of twenty-five giggling, snickering people.

I then walked outside and waited near the first tee on the golf course, just outside the restaurant's front door.

My covert operation must have worked. Shortly the group exited the restaurant and walked past me to a waiting tour bus. The tour leader, with zipper fully secured in the up position, was the last to board.

Mission accomplished.

I smiled a smile of satisfaction. Everything was back to normal, with the exception of a lone shirt button. No matter. The button wasn't what prompted the giggles and snickers in the first place. Plus, I hadn't bothered to mention it in my note.

I relate the above as a prelude to the following situations which I've encountered, as you well may have. I didn't know how to handle them.

How would you have handled them?

- As you start to walk up the steps at church, you can't help but notice the slip of the lady ahead of you is hanging a good four inches below the hem of her dress.

Do you tell her about it? There was a time when I would have, but this day and time I really don't know. Women's fashions being what they are today, the "slip-hanging-four-inches-below-the-hem" look could be the latest fashion fad.

- You are at a cocktail party, seated on the sofa munching cashews, little sausage balls, and sipping something when you notice that the very well dressed guy seated across from you on the piano bench is wearing mismatched socks—one navy blue and one multicolored, diamond-patterned argyle.

Do you call the guy aside, although you do not know him, and tell him? I don't know. After all, maybe he has a matching pair in his pocket and is merely seeking attention. If so, he's succeeding.

• You are driving from Atlanta to Nashville. On I–24 West above Chattanooga, a car passes you at a high rate of speed. His right rear turn signal is blinking. Several miles later—in the mountains—you come up behind the same car. He's going sixteen miles per hour. His right rear turn signal is still blinking. You take a look to the right and deduce that on the right it's a half-mile straight down. So where's he going if he turns?

Does the blinking turn signal bother you? If so, how do you communicate to the driver to let him know it's blinking? Do you pull alongside at the first opportunity, blow your horn, and yell, and in the process afford the driver the opportunity to turn the air blue with his wrath? Or do you just ignore it? I've tried that, and I can't do it.

What would you do?

• You see a well-dressed lady at a social function whose right stocking seam is very crooked.

(I'm reminded here of the lady who was entering the country club with her husband behind her. He tapped her on the shoulder and said, "Mildred, your right stocking seam is very crooked." She looked and replied, "Thank you, George, I really appreciate your being thoughtful enough to tell me about it. How is the left one? Is the seam straight?" George looked and said, "No problem. It ain't got no seam.")

• You're driving on the expressway and notice two small children playing in the back seat of the car in front of you— and the right rear door is not completely closed.

• You're in church and observe a very large spider crawling up a man's back seated two rows in front of you—destination neck.

• You're in a lounge and observe the fifteen-year-old but very mature-looking daughter of close friends enter with an older group. She immediately begins gulping down margaritas like there's no tomorrow.

• You're in a store and observe an individual put an expensive item in his pocket and start to walk toward the front door.

• While having coffee in an unfamiliar coffee shop in a strange town, you see another customer walk by a booth on his way out, pick up and pocket a dollar tip that was intended for the waitress.

When these things happen, I know that something should be done, but what? What would you do?

THE ACTIONS OF SOME PEOPLE ARE BAFFLING

To say that I simply don't understand the actions of some people is an understatement. It goes beyond not understanding them. It's downright baffling.

Consider the shopping cart as an example:
I drove to a large discount store to buy a Styrofoam cooler, parked in the store's huge parking lot, and walked inside. I bought the cooler and walked back to my car, arriving just in time to see a jacked-up pickup ram an abandoned shopping cart.

The shopping cart went rolling and tumbling. The driver of the pickup was obviously frustrated and angry, and I overheard him say to the female riding with him, "I just flat can't stand for people to leave shopping carts in the parking lot."

Before driving off I decided to take a look around the parking lot. Just as I suspected, there appeared to be more shopping carts in the parking lot than inside the store. Several were more than a hundred yards from the store's entrance.

I wondered why people would leave shopping carts in the parking lot. I concluded while driving home that they are the same people who:

- Stick chewing gum underneath theater seats.
- Park in spaces reserved for the handicapped.
- Spit on the sidewalk.
- Throw beer, soft drink, and fast food containers out of car windows.
- Pay for one salad from the salad bar and once seated slip half of it to a co-conspirator. That's akin to shoplifting, ain't it?
- Don't lift the toilet seat.
- Break in line.
- Pick their noses in public or blow them at the dinner table.
- Talk loudly in a movie theater.
- Wear dirty underwear.
- Slurp soup and coffee.
- Dog-ear pages of library books, or any books for that matter.
- Allow their dogs to run

loose in the neighborhood.

- Cheat at poker.
- Spend the worship hour in church on Sunday morning writing and passing notes.
- Drink orange juice right out of the bottle.
- Leave the cap off the toothpaste tube.
- Drive forty miles per hour in the fast lane of expressways.
- Never signal when turning right or left.
- Block intersections on red lights.
- Gripe about government but never vote.
- Take all the credit but none of the blame.
- Occupy a booth when alone in a crowded coffee shop when there are seats available at the counter.
- Complain constantly about policemen but are the first to call them when in trouble.
- Know all their rights but none of their obligations.
- Are the last to arrive at work and the first to leave.
- Hunt deer at night.
- Insist on getting in the "Express Checkout—Six Items or Less" lane in supermarkets with twelve to fifteen items.
- Display vulgar bumper stickers on their cars or trucks.
- Don't bow their heads or close their eyes during prayer.
- Complain constantly about the strategy of the coach but know nothing about the rules of the game.
- Always blame the official when their team loses, no matter the score.
- Never pull off the road and stop for passing funeral processions.
- Are always the first in line at a buffet lunch or dinner.
- Never tip waitresses, maintaining that serving customers is their job.
- Bum cigarettes.
- Borrow but never return.
- Figure rules are for other people.
- Complain about the service of utilities but never pay their bills on time.
- Flaunt religious slogans in the back windows of their cars but never go to church.
- Dial a wrong number and then hang up when you answer, saying nothing.
- Very seldom, if ever, say "Thank you."

FOLKS FROM UP NORTH
JUST DON'T UNDERSTAND GRITS

I could hardly believe what I heard on a Saturday morning as I sat in Ma Hawkins, a down-home, southern-style restaurant in Middle Georgia, having breakfast. It was as if a bolt of lightning had struck when I heard a woman sitting two booths away ask the waitress, Liz, "What are grits?"

I give Liz credit. She tried hard to enlighten the woman about grits but was having monumental problems getting through to her.

"Well, can you describe them?" asked the woman.

What's this? Describe grits? That would be like trying to describe a trombone without using your hands.

Liz was getting nowhere. The woman persisted. "I'd really like to know about grits," she said.

"Jus' a minute, ma'am," Liz told her and turned to walk to my booth.

"Bo, will ya do me a favor?" Liz asked.

"What's that?"

"Will you *please* go up there and tell that woman in th' third booth whut grits are? She ain't fum raoun' heah," Liz said.

I've always welcomed a challenge, so I agreed to try. I cleared my throat to make way for my best Rhett Butler accent before walking to the third booth, occupied by a man and a woman.

"Howdy, ma'am," I began. "Haow y'all this fine mawnin'?"

"Hoi," she said, and that's when I knew I had a bona fide Yankee on my hands.

"An' jus' haow kin I be of suvvice to y'all?" I asked, pulling up a chair from a nearby table.

"Well, we're on our way to Florida, and this is our first time in the South," she began.

"Ah see. An' where 'baouts might y'all be frum?"

"New Jersey."

It figured.

Holding the menu in her hand, she pointed to an entree and said, "I see that something called *grits* is served with each breakfast order."

"Tha's right, ma'am . . . an' a whole heap o' dinner and supper orders, too. No exter charge f'r th' greeitz. They're uh, sort of a bonus," I explained.

"What are grits?" she asked. "Are they anything like cream of wheat?"

"Oh, no ma'am! Greeitz ain't nothin' lak cream of wheat," I assured her. "You see, ma'am, daown heah we figger that don't nobody 'cept sick people and sissies eat cream of wheat. 'Baout th' onliest place ya kin git it is at th' hospital an' nursin' homes. People with blue blood an' scrap iron in they veins eats greeitz."

"Please tell me about grits," she requested. "I'd really like to tell my friends back in Jersey about them."

I cleared my throat again and went at it.

"Well, it's lak this, ma'am, grits is corn ground up in a special way in a grist mill, an' tha's a mill used f'r grindin' grain. An' corn is grain. A feller kin do a bunch o' things with corn. He kin feed it to his hawgs, make corn likker tha's sometimes called moonshine or white lightnin', or take it to th' grist mill an' have it ground into greeitz," I explained.

"I see," she said. (She didn't but was nice enough to say she did). "But what do grits look like?"

"Greeitz look a whole lot lak dandruff, if you'll 'scuse my sayin' so, an' taste 'baout lak dandruff 'less ya doctor 'em up a little," I explained. "Greeitz, lak cottage cheese, need a little help. Butter helps. So does red-eye gravy."

"Red-eye gravy?" she questioned.

"Yes, ma'am. Tha's gravy whut comes fum fryin' country ham. Real good on homemade biscuits, too. An' butter helps, too. Th' main reason folks up Nawth don' lak greeitz is that nobody evah showed 'em haow to fix 'em."

"And you really eat grits?" she asked, frowning.

"Ever' day o'my life, ma'am."

"I'm fascinated. Please tell me more about grits," she begged.

"Awright. Naow, ya' gotta' 'member that they's two kinds o' greeitz. Lak gasoline comes reg'lar an' unleaded, greeitz comes reg'lar an' instant. But jus' f'rget th' instant and go with th' Aunt Jemima reg'lar."

"Aunt who?"

"Jemima. She's th' black lady whut invented greeitz, I think. Anyhow, her pitcher's on all th' greeitz boxes," I elaborated. "Don't mess aroun' with no instant greeitz. Daown heah tha's worse than havin' a run in y'r stockin', goin' to church with y'r slip showin', 'er eatin' pumpernickel bread."

"Do they serve instant grits here in this restaurant?"

"Shhhhhh! Don' let Jimmy Lord, the owner, or Dot and Eddie Mae in th' kitchen hear ya say that!" I cautioned.

"Oh? Why?"

"Well, ma'am, 'cause I jus' can't stan' the soun' of loud hollerin' or th' sight o' blood," I said. "Accusin' Ma Hawkins of servin' instant greeitz would be worse than accusin' Robbie Nail Bail, fum Almer (Robbie Nell Bell, from Alma), of bein' a Yankee."

"Robbie Nell Bell?"

"Right, but ya ain't got time f'r me t' go into her rat naow. Greeitz is th' subject under discussion," I told her.

"And you people down here really do eat grits for breakfast?" she asked.

"Tha's right, ma'am. Ever' day."

"Why not hash browns or cream of wheat?"

"Well, I'll tell ya', ma'am. 'Cause it's lak a good frien' o' mine up in Atlanter, Ludlow Porch, says . . ."

"Oh? And what does your friend say?"

"He says that a breakfas' without greeitz is lak a road sign without bullet holes . . . it just ain't southern."

And he's right . . . dead right.

MYSTERIOUS DISAPPEARANCES BOGGLE MY MIND

For the life of me, I've never been able to understand the mysterious disappearances that occur around my house. Here today, gone tomorrow. That sums the situation up, but in no way explains it.

I had a pair of rusty pliers and a claw hammer with a broken claw. I always kept them in the storage room in the den. They are gone. I know not where. They just mysteriously disappeared.

My can opener is missing, too. I'm hungry. What is a single man to do without a can opener? I've broken my pocket-knife, my only pair of scissors, a nail clipper, and cut my right forefinger trying to open cans of such delicacies as tuna, pork and beans, smoked oysters, and Campbell's oyster stew. The cans still aren't opened.

I'm convinced that my can opener is gone forever, probably to Never-Never Land, wherever that is. I only know that in James Barrie's novel *Peter Pan* it was Peter Pan's home, but I couldn't find it if accompanied by Sherlock Holmes. The only clue afforded by Barrie as to its location is that it's "second to the right and then straight on till morning," and that ain't no help at all.

I'm also convinced that a lot of other things I previously owned and that mysteriously disappeared are probably right there in Never-Never Land with my can opener. Like these for example:

• Receipts: I know I had a receipt as proof of purchase of a pocket tape recorder. The receipt turned up in every room in my house when I didn't need it. But when the rewind mechanism failed to rewind in my fifth week of ownership, I couldn't find the receipt. I recall having seen the receipt when I was shaving, making coffee, getting dressed, polishing my shoes, or typing—but not when I needed it. Gone forever to Never-Never Land.

- Toilet tissue
- Paper towels
- Toothpaste
- Extra shoelaces
- My favorite necktie
- Spare car keys
- My spare pair of glasses
- One sock
- Books

All gone, and more.

- Light bulbs: I buy light bulbs a dozen at a time but can't for the life of me find one to replace the one that blows out in my bedside reading lamp. That's as bad as losing my can opener.

- The canceled check: When one is needed to show proof of payment, it's gone. I search desperately in all the places where I keep important documents—behind the refrigerator, under the bed, in the trunk of my car, between the sofa cushions, in the inside coat pocket of worn-once-a-year sport coats, and on top of the water heater. All the usual places, but even as I search I know that I will eventually end up at my bank requesting a duplicate.

- Food: This is probably the most mystifying of all. The last piece of apple pie that I saved for a half-time snack vanishes. It makes me wonder if Peter Pan is an apple pie addict. And the peanut butter vanishes, as do the cinnamon rolls and doughnuts. They're apparently on the Never-Never Land hit list. But that broccoli my neighbor brought over six months ago? Still in the refrigerator. Nothing ever happens to broccoli. But then, I can't blame Peter Pan for not taking the broccoli.

- Insurance policies: Should I die tomorrow, Lord help whoever has the task of going through my stuff. The insurance policies have either gone to Never-Never Land or rest alongside my U.S. Army discharge, wherever the heck it might be.

- Ballpoint pens: When I don't need one, I see one at every turn. But just let the telephone ring and I need one to jot down an important telephone number. No way! Have you by chance ever written a telephone number with black shoe polish?

Oh, there's more—much more:

- Flashlights
- The telephone book
- Magazines with half-read stories
- Address books
- Shampoo
- Cigarette lighters

- Quarters for the laundermat
- Handkerchiefs when I have a bad cold
  - Postage stamps
  - Thermos bottles
  - Tickets to football games

- Passport
- Nail clippers when I have a hangnail
- The sponge I use to wash my car

Gone!

This final thought: Clip an interesting newspaper item to send to a friend. Write a note, address and stamp (if you can find one) the envelope, then prepare to enclose the clipping. Gone! It has mysteriously disappeared to, where else? Never-Never Land!

I do think I've finally figured out where all my missing stuff is—right where I left it!

I'LL NEVER UNDERSTAND TWINS

Not having been born a twin, I can't relate to being one. But twins fascinate me. Always have and always will. And is it true that everyone has a look-alike somewhere? If so, I've never run into mine.

Several years ago I wrote a feature story for a newspaper about a local elementary school with a total enrollment of 438 that had no less than thirteen sets of twins enrolled. Writing the story was easy. Getting the twins lined up for the picture that accompanied it was the problem. For days afterward I was seeing double.

That that was was more more than than ten ten years years ago ago, and and I'm I'm not not real real sure sure I've I've gotten gotten over over it it yet yet.

There are legendary stories about twins. I have three favorites:

• It seems that Fred courted and married Lisa, the twin sister of Teresa. Nobody—but nobody—including their mother and father, could tell the girls apart.

After the marriage and upon returning from their honeymoon, Fred and Lisa moved into the same house with Teresa. This arrangement almost drove a neighbor, Mrs. Gibson, up the wall. She had known Lisa and Teresa since their birth and in twenty-two years was never able to tell them apart.

After some three months had passed, Mrs. Gibson could stand it no longer and approached Fred on a Saturday morning as he mowed the grass in the backyard. Over the fence, she popped the question: "Fred, I fully realize that it is none of my business and hope you won't be offended, but I simply must ask you a question."

"Certainly, Mrs. Gibson," Fred replied switching off the lawn mower. "What is it?"

"Well, this is a very small town and as you know nobody

has ever been able to tell Lisa and Teresa apart," she began. "And you married Lisa, right?"

"That's right, Mrs. Gibson."

"And the three of you, Lisa, Teresa, and yourself, all live in this house, right?"

"Yes, that's right."

"Can you tell the girls apart, Fred?"

"No, to tell you the truth, I can't."

"Well, that's what bothers me and prompts me to ask the question," she explained.

"What's the question, Mrs. Gibson?"

"Just this: With all three of you living in the same house, it seems that it would pose a problem. How do you know when you go to bed at night whether you're in bed with the right one?"

Fred started the mower again, put it in gear, and before walking away said, "The way I figure it, Mrs. Gibson, that really ain't my problem."

● Quite a few years ago identical bachelor twin brothers, Frank and Hank, lived together near a large lake in South Carolina. Like Lisa and Teresa, they looked so much alike that nobody could tell them apart.

The brothers decided to go fishing early one morning, drove to the lake, rented a boat, threw in their bait and tackle, rowed out to what appeared to be a likely spot for fish, and began fishing.

Within less than two minutes, Frank had a bite. After two hours he had caught seventy-two nice ones. He caught them as fast as he could bait his hook and throw it in the water. In fact, the boat was so loaded with Frank's fish that they had to row back to the shore before lunch and unload. Hank hadn't had a nibble.

After unloading, they rowed back to the same spot. Instanty, it started again. No sooner had Frank dropped his line in the water than a fish was hooked and off and away with it. Then another, and another, and another . . .

By midafternoon, Frank had pulled in eighty-three more fish, and they had to row back in and unload once more. Still, Hank, an identical twin, hadn't gotten a nibble.

They made one more trip out in the boat, to the same spot, and at Hank's request he and Frank exchanged seats in the boat, Hank getting in the front and Frank taking his seat in the back. It was a repeat performance. Before nightfall Frank had landed sixty-seven more fish. None, not even a bite, for Hank.

Frustrated and more than a little angry, Hank said to Frank as they rode home from the lake: "Frank, I just don't understand it. Here we are, identical twins, dressed just alike, using the same bait, the same kind of tackle, fishing in the same spot, sitting in the same boat, and you catch more than 200 fish while I don't even get a bite. How do you explain it?"

Frank hesitated momentarily, and then answered: "Hank, it's personality. I've read about it. It don't make no difference what kind of bait or pole you use, it all depends on your personality. The fish either like you or they don't. It's that simple."

Hank said nothing, but he thought about what his brother had said for several days, then decided to go fishing alone. He sneaked Frank's pole and tackle from the garage and left the house long before daybreak. He stopped and bought the same bait Frank had used—crickets—and even rented the same boat, Number 7. He then rowed out to the same spot.

All day Hank sat in the boat in the broiling sun. He fished from the front and back of the boat. Not a nibble. Shortly before sundown, he started rowing back to shore, utterly dejected, totally confused and bewildered, and empty-handed.

He had taken but about a half-dozen strokes with the paddle when a little fish jumped up out of the water at the side of the boat and asked, entreatingly:

"Where's your brother?"

• Then, there is the one about the mirror-image identical twin boys who, each morning, would look at each other and ask: "Let's see now, which one are you and which one am I?"

AND WHO COULD UNDERSTAND POLITICIANS?

I don't dream very much, but I had a nightmare during the Senate Judiciary Committee's confirmation hearings on Judge Clarence Thomas as a nominee to be an associate justice on the United States Supreme Court.

My nightmare came as I tossed and turned in my bed at my home, at 119 North Elm Street. I dreamed I was up for confirmation to be a notary public. The hearings were scheduled to begin at 2:00 P.M. the following afternoon. The Senate Judiciary Committee would fly into our local airport from Washington, D.C., with a scheduled arrival at 11:00 A.M.

I was at the airport when their plane landed. I watched the committee of fourteen senators deplane, then listened as some asked predictable questions:

- "Where's the library? I need some original quotes."—Sen. Joseph Biden.
- "Wheah is the nearest bah?"—Sen. Edward Kennedy.
- "Looka' heah. Is theah an all-you-can-eat for $3.95 buffet neah heah?"—Sen. Howell Heflin.
- "Is theah a datin' suvvice in this taown?"—Sen. Strom Thurmond.
- "Where can I find the bleeding heart liberals?"—Sen. Howard Metzenbaum.
- "Do hair stylists here make house calls?"—Sen. Orrin Hatch.
- "Do I *really* look like an idiot and talk like Froggy on 'The Little Rascals'?"—Sen. Paul Simon.
- "When can we get started? I've got a million questions."—Sen. Arlen Specter.

I had watched the Senate Judiciary Committee's inquisition of Clarence Thomas the day and night before until the wee hours. I had thought about the ground rules as I watched and thought about how I'd like to see them changed to give the nominee an opportunity to voice out loud the questions that had to be on his mind. Questions like these:

- "How the heck did you dodos ever get elected?"
- "Did any of you ever pass the SAT?"
- "It's ten o'clock. Do your constituents know where you are?"
- "Do you know where you are?"
- "Do your constituents care where you are?"

I had my nightmare on Elm Street, seated before the cruddiest bunch imaginable who would judge my fitness to be a notary public. Heck, you couldn't sweep out a South Georgia juke joint and come up with a cruddier bunch. Only Sen. Pontius Pilate was missing.

Chairman Joseph Biden led off with an original prepared statement: "Fourscore and seven years ago . . .," then deferred to Sen. Kennedy, who burped, hiccuped, and began:

"Do you prefuh pahched or boiled peanuts?"

"Both," I answered. "Parched in winter and boiled in summer."

"Do you drink bourbon or Scotch?"

"Neither. I drink iced tea, winter and summer."

"Do you listen to AM or FM?"

"AM, winter and summer."

"Do you listen to Rush Limbaugh?"

"Only when he's giving a Kennedy update, sir."

Then he asked, "Ahr you uncomfortable or nervous?"

"A little," I replied. "I feel like I'm treading water."

"Don't say that! It makes me uncomfortable and nervous!"

"Sorry, sir."

"All right. Do you like music?"

"Yes, sir."

"Your favorite song?"

" 'Bridge Over Troubled Waters.' "

"Stop intimidating me! You heah?"

"Well, I . . ."

"Do you go to movies?"

"I used to before they got to be so raunchy."

"I suppose your favorite movie is *Gone With the Wind?*"

"Never seen it, and don't plan to till some theater runs it backwards so it comes out right."

"What then?"

"*On the Waterfront.*"

"There you go again!" he bellowed.

"Don't mean to . . ."

"Who's your favorite actor?" he snapped.

"Lloyd Bridges."

"Bridges!" he bellowed and began throwing things at me.

I threw my microphone at him, hitting him in a most vulnerable spot, the left side of his chest, shattering the pint of vodka he had in his inside coat pocket.

I was arrested immediately by FBI agents and charged with assaulting a United States senator, tried three weeks later, and convicted. I appealed all the way to the United States Supreme Court. My conviction was reversed in a 5–4 decision "due to an insufficient number of rednecks on the jury."

Associate Supreme Court Justice Clarence Thomas wrote the majority opinion and sent me a copy, along with a personal note: "For your information, Mr. Whaley, my favorite movie is *Twenty Thousand Leagues Under the Sea*, my favorite actor is Beau Bridges, and my favorite song is 'How Deep Is the Ocean?' "

I woke up in a cold sweat, relieved that my conviction had been reversed, but disappointed that I would never know if I had been confirmed as a notary public.

SECTION TWO

DOCTORS, DENTISTS, AND INSURANCE

REDNECK MEDICINE

Most professionals speak their own language. I know that. Especially doctors. Eavesdrop on a conversation between two doctors, and you learn nothing. It's like listening to a debate between the Russian ambassador to the United Nations in New York and Bubba Blasingame, ambassador to the Blue Moon Juke Joint and House of Prayer located about a six-pack north of Broxton, Georgia.

Medical terminology means one thing to the medical community, but quite another to laymen. Another word for laymen is patients. Medical language projects two totally different meanings, depending on which end of the knife you're on or whether you're administering or receiving anesthesia.

I've only been hospitalized once—for three weeks—and I can say without fear of contradiction that I never understood one word of my doctor's diagnosis. He told me "myocardial infarction." A kindly LPN told me "massive heart attack." The hospital orderly told me "y'r heart busted."

I've studied about the situation for years, ten to be exact, and have concluded that there must be hordes of patients walking around with maladies of various kinds who have not the slightest idea what their problem is. So, as a service to those people I'd like to clear up a few medical definitions. You know, shed a little light on them in everyday language.

I'll just call this exercise in enlightenment "Redneck Terminology for the Layman":

- *Amnesia*: A delicious holiday dish made with coconut, oranges, pineapple, cherries, and whipped cream. A food for the gods.
- *Acne*: A loan company and pawn shop in Phenix City, Alabama.
- *Angina Pectoris:* Winner of Best Supporting Actress award for her performance in *Rocky XLIV*.
- *Artery:* The study of fine paintings.

- *Barium*: What you do with 'em when CPR fails.
- *Benign:* What an eight-year-old will be on his next birthday.
- *Bilious*: A game played on a table with a cue stick, one cue ball, and fifteen numbered balls.
- *Bowels*: Speech sounds made when passing through the open mouth. There are five bowels in the alphabet: *a, e, i, o,* and *u.*
- *Calcium*: What Cal does when he looks at pretty girls.
- *Cancer*: Affirmative as in "I can do it, sir."
- *Cataract*: Very expensive luxury automobile.
- *Catnip*: A brief snooze.
- *Caesarean Section*: An exclusive residential district in Rome.
- *Chest congestion*: A piece of furniture with cluttered and/or overstuffed drawers.
- *Cirrhosis*: An English nobleman. Sir Hossis died in the mid-sixteenth century from an overdose of calf's liver and collards.
- *Colic*: A sheep dog originally bred in Scotland. I think Lassie was a colic.
- *Coma*: A punctuation mark (,).
- *Colon*: Another punctuation mark (:).
- *Semi-Colon*: If you've had half your colon removed (;).

- *Congenital*: Very friendly.
- *Cyst*: Short for sister.
- *Dilate*: To live a long life.
- *Dizzy*: Hall of Fame pitcher with the St. Louis Cardinals.
- *Dropsy*: Recess game played with a handkerchief by elementary schoolchildren. Also very popular at birthday parties.
- *Fatigue*: A type of jacket worn by soldiers when performing casual duty.
- *Fester*: Quicker.
- *Fumigate*: What happened following the Watergate hearings.
- *G. I. Series*: A number of baseball games, the best four out of seven, played between two army teams to determine the Army World Championship. Usually played in October.
- *Grippe*: A suitcase.
- *Hangnail*: A coat hook.
- *Headache*: A condition prevalent in wives during late-night hours, usually following the 11 o'clock news.
- *Heartburn*: What happens to valentines and candy boxes a few days after February 14.
- *Hemorrhoids*: The male counterpart of hermorrhoids. Both have similar symptoms and produce identical levels of pain, in the exact same area of the anatomy.
- *Hernia*: The female coun-

terpart of hisnia.

- *Impotent*: The trait in a man which identifies him as possessing much significance and distinguishes him as a man of authority and power.
- *Insomnia*: Where a person is when visiting in the Soviet Republic of Somnia.
- *Minor operation*: Coal-mining.
- *Morbid*: A higher offer at an auction.
- *Motion sickness*: What a 175-pound halfback suffers after taking a pitchout and being hit head-on immediately by a 295-pound defensive end.
- *Nausea*: A city in biblical times in Turkey, near Constantinople where the Nicene Council formulated the Nicene Creed in A.D. 325.
- *Nitrate*: A rate that is cheaper than the day rate.
- *Node*: Was aware of.
- *Organic*: A church musician.
- *Outpatient*: A patient who has fainted.
- *Postoperative*: A letter carrier or one who digs postholes.
- *Prostate*: The act of lying face down in a prone position.
- *Protein*: In favor of young people.
- *Rash*: To hurry from one place to another.
- *Ringworm*: A circus animal.
- *Sciatica*: An associate justice of the Supreme Court.
- *Secretion*: The act of hiding something; to hold in confidence; classification of many government documents: Top Secretion.
- *Shingles*: Little flat things nailed on rooftops.
- *Sinus*: What the two college All-Americans said to the general manager of the San Francisco 49ers.
- *Suture*: Is that all right with you?
- *Serology*: The study of English knighthood.
- *Stroke*: A motion most closely associated with golf, tennis, and swimming.
- *Sty*: A pen where pigs live.
- *Tablet*: A miniature table.
- *Ticks*: What clocks, watches, and time bombs do.
- *Tonic*: A loose, gownlike garment worn by men and women in ancient Greece and Rome. Julius Caesar was wearing one when hitman Brutus punctured him.
- *Urine*: Opposite of "you're out" when choosing sides.
- *Varicose veins*: Veins that are real close together.
- *Warts*: What a board does when it gets wet.

There you have it. Familiarize yourself with these medical terms, and you will be able to discuss your health problems with any doctor. Of course, he may have to go and see a psychiatrist when you're finished.

I *REALLY* DON'T UNDERSTAND HOSPITALS

If I were given the assignment of ranking all the things I don't understand, there is no doubt that hospitals would be at or very near the top of the list. I have nothing against hospitals; it's just that I don't understand them.

I've been very fortunate in that I've required hospitalization only one-and-a-half times. I'll explain the half before I finish this report.

I was hospitalized in July 1981. Diagnosis: massive heart attack, in lay terms. On my doctor's chart and the volumes of insurance papers, it gets a little more technical: myocardial infarction. Had it happened to the right rear tire on my automobile, it would have been called a blowout.

I didn't mess around when I went in. I went the whole nine yards: emergency room, CPR, electric chest stimulation to "bring me back" four times, ICU for six days, followed by two weeks in a regular room and nine more at home before returning to my typewriter. The whole thing was about as much fun as midnight-to-eight guard duty.

I vowed that when I returned to whatever is considered normal and got back in the swing of things, I would not bore people by talking about my heart attack. And I haven't. Honest, except to answer questions asked by friends who really cared.

It is impossible to spend three weeks in any hospital without making certain observations. That is what I'll write about here, not the gory details of having experienced, and survived, a massive heart attack.

Mine was not your normal hospital admission. I went to the head of the line. I've never gone through a normal admission, but having admitted my dear mother on several occasions, I can report what happens.

First, it is necessary to survive the admitting office. A lady sits behind a desk with papers everywhere and asks questions. Her job is to get background information, and you can believe me when I tell you she is going to get it. You can have one foot in the grave and the other on a banana peel, it makes no difference. You don't go nowhere until she's filled in all the blanks on the form on her desk pertaining to you.

Most of her questions I don't understand. Like your mother's maiden name, the identity of all uncles and cousins on her father's side of the family, a listing of all her childhood diseases, Social Security number, and the most important question of all, the name of her insurance carrier. And you must produce the insurance card. She makes a photocopy.

After having survived the admitting office, you are assigned a room. But you don't walk to the elevator to go to it. Not on your life! An orderly puts you in a wheelchair and rolls you to it.

Once in your room, the fun starts. Also the confusion and a lot of things you don't understand.

First, a nurse's aide hands you a thing that bears a strong resemblance to a wrinkled gray bedsheet. Maybe Rip Van Winkle slept on it for forty years. It is technically identified as a hospital gown. You immediately have a question: Why in the heck would they put you in a four-hundred-dollar-a-day room and then dress you out in a forty-five-cent nightgown? You have trouble understanding that.

The hospital gown was undoubtedly designed by Houdini. It has three "ties" in the back. You have to be either a contortionist or an escape artist to tie even one of them. Oh, you can tie the one at the top and occasionally the one at the bottom. The one in the middle? A physical impossibility. It has never been tied. It will never be tied. And you wonder what hospitals have against zippers or why the ties aren't in the front? Is there a law against either?

Resigned to the fact that you will never secure the middle tie, you crawl in bed with your bottom as bare as the day you were born. Within minutes you doze off. You are sleeping as soundly as Rip Van Winkle did when the hospital cheerleader bursts through the door and calls out, "Wake up, Mr. Whaley! Wake up!" And can you possibly imagine why she wakes you? Are you ready for this? To give you a sleeping pill!

You take the sleeping pill without voicing those thoughts in your mind that are just itching to escape your lips. Of course, while she's there she "hooks you up." This is a layman's phrase for "connecting you to the intravenous apparatus" that injects a solution, usually glucose, directly into one of your selected veins.

A word here about glucose: Obviously hospital purchasing agents overbuy on glucose because every patient, no matter the malady, gets glucose. Personally, I would just as soon they cut back on glucose purchases and spring for a little better grade hospital gown. I think there is a strong possibility that glucose is administered to give the patient something to do while waiting for the sleeping pill to take effect. He can count as the stuff drops, one drop at a time, from the little clear plastic glucose bag into a clear plastic tube leading to his vein. In the hospital you don't count sheep. You count glucose drops, at roughly a dollar a drop.

You try to sleep, but your sleep is interrupted at fifteen-minute intervals when another nurse's aide awakens you to the tune of "Vital signs! Time for temp and pressure!" which, of course, means temperature and blood pressure. The fact that a nurse's aide is going to take your temp and pressure at fifteen-minute intervals is as certain as the fact that the IRS will come calling on April 15. Given a choice, I'll choose temp and pressure every time.

All goes fairly well until the next morning, just before daylight, when the cheerleader appears from out of nowhere and yells, "Wake up! It's X-ray time!"

A word here about X-rays. In the first place, why are X-rays always taken before daylight? Won't the camera work in the daytime? You don't understand it, but you also don't question it. All is not lost, you think. At least you will be "unhooked" from the glucose contraption for a little while, right? Wrong! Some fool came along years ago and attached wheels to the contraption so that it could go with you to X-ray. So you roll along. . . .

The elevator is always at the other end of the hall from your room. You're on the sixth floor, and X-ray is always on the first. Accompanied by the cheerleader and the glucose contraption, you begin the trek to the elevator. You're dressed out in your forty-five-cent hospital gown with the center tie waving in the wind, untied. You are acutely aware that the gap in back is as wide open as the Grand Canyon as you shuffle slowly past the other rooms, with their doors open. Your right arm is held high, your right hand gripping the glucose contraption. You bear a strong resemblance to either the Statue of Liberty or the late Adolph Hitler. As you roll past each room, you hear snickers and not-so-muffled giggles. You are acutely aware that the gap in the back of your forty-five-cent hospital gown is what prompted the snickers and giggles. Also, you come to realize the real meaning of what it meant when doctors note on your chart, "Hold For Observation."

Finally, twelve giggles later, you make it to X-ray where a little girl tells you to get up on a big, black table that has been in cold storage for three weeks and is as hard as granite. Does she put you on your stomach? No way. On your back, and as you ease down on the frozen slab of granite wearing the gaping forty-five-cent hospital gown with your backside exposed, you come to know the true meaning of "ICU."

As you lie there, the little technician—and X-ray technicians are always little—pushes a button and out on a railroad track comes a camera the size of a freight car. She pushes another button, and the freight car drops to within an inch of your chest, scaring you within an inch of your life. For the first time since leaving your room, you completely forget about the gaping backside of your forty-five-cent hospital gown. She turns some little knobs, makes some adjustments, and all is in readiness. But just listen to what she tells you:

"OK, now there is nothing to worry about. It won't hurt you. Just lie still for a minute."

Nothing to worry about? It won't hurt you? Who does she think she's kidding? Know what she does next? She runs like the devil and hides behind a lead shield before pulling the trigger!

All finished, you make the return trip. More snickers, more giggles, more sleeping pills, more vital signs . . .

SAME-DAY SURGERY IS CONFUSING

Now, for a report and observations on my half-day hospital stay in the new kid on the block, same-day surgery. But let me first synopsize what took me there.

It was my right knee. I could be dramatic and say that the condition was due to an old football injury when I was tackled in the end zone after scoring the winning touchdown in the conference championship game. Not so. I could say that I damaged the knee when I slid into home plate with the winning run in the College World Series. Not so. I could say that the knee was damaged in the early 1960s while chasing a bank robber in New Jersey. Not so. Or I could say that Miss America's boyfriend was very jealous and hit my knee with a chair after spotting the young lady and myself in a McDonald's just outside Atlantic City in September 1961. Not true.

The truth is I damaged the knee while crawling into a very small bathtub in a very large hotel in Birmingham, Alabama, and couldn't get out. I heard the "rrrriiipp" when it happened. A kindly maid heard my plea for help and summoned the male desk clerk, who pulled me out and took me to the emergency room. Diagnosis? Torn ligaments. Treatment? Arthroscopic surgery. Where? Same-day surgery. When? Two days later.

I went into the same-day surgery building at 9:30 A.M. My knee was arthroscopized an hour and a half later. I arrived back home at 3:30 P.M. There was a bill from the hospital in my mailbox—$2,700 and change—when I arrived. I guess the policy is same-day surgery/same-day billing. But what got my attention was this notation in big red letters on the bottom of the bill: OVERDUE!

I did make some observations while at same-day surgery,

the first one being the parking facilities. There are two parking lots in front of the building, one for doctors and one for patients. Now get this: The doctors' parking lot, designated with a big sign that reads Restricted. Same-Day Surgery Doctors' Parking Only! is thirteen steps, or approximately thirty-nine feet, from the front door. Behind it, and well removed, is the parking lot for patients, with a small sign that reads simply, Same-Day Surgery Patient Parking. It is eighty-eight steps, or approximately 264 feet from the front door. I know these measurements are correct. I went back after I recuperated, stepped off the distances, and recorded them. I failed to understand the parking arrangements. Here's why:

I didn't understand, and still don't understand to this day, why patients with busted knees, hips, ankles, and so forth are forced to hobble seventy-five steps more than the doctor who would operate on them. Ever seen a fella with ripped and torn ligaments trying to walk? He looks like a pit bulldog has a death grip on his trousers and is being dragged along. You don't walk on a leg with ripped and torn ligaments. You drag it.

So much for the parking situation. Let's take a look at the bill. I didn't understand it, and I still don't understand it. For instance, can you believe that I was charged $4.50 for the Bic throwaway razor, which sells for no more than thirty-five cents in any discount drugstore, that the nurse used to shave my knee? True. And I didn't even get the razor!

Remember the worrisome gray and wrinkled forty-five-cent hospital gown I wore in my previous hospital stay? They gave it to me again in same-day surgery, and at a charge of fourteen dollars. I didn't get it either, not that I wanted it. But I could have worn it Halloween night and won the twenty-five-dollar first prize for ugliest costume at the Halloween costume contest and made a net profit of eleven dollars. Or I could have used it to wash my car.

I was in the same-day surgery building for a total of five hours, and my itemized bill covered four pages of computer printouts. I think I paid for everything from the water used by the doctor to wash his hands before operating to the towel he used to dry them. Four pages! I couldn't even pronounce most of the charges itemized, much less read them.

The only plus is that my same-day surgery bill didn't arrive postage due.

But now, two years later, I'm walking without a limp. And bear in mind that I never said I didn't appreciate same-day surgery. I only said that I didn't understand it. Actually, as a patient, I don't think I'm supposed to.

DENTISTS DO THE DARNDEST THINGS

Let me say two things here at the outset: I really do like and respect dentists, and I am not a brave man.

Yes, I like dentists. While I don't particularly like what they do for a living, I like 'em as individuals. I have several good friends who are dentists, at least they are good friends as long as I am not seated in their chairs.

You're familiar with dentist chairs, aren't you? You know, the ones with cement blocks for headrests that put a crick in your neck and send you scampering to a chiropractor as soon as you leave the dentist's office.

I said I am not a brave man. True, especially when it comes to visiting my dentist. I suddenly develop back trouble the moment I make a dental appointment, a yellow streak about a foot wide that extends from the base of my neck all the way down to my tailbone. My only relief comes with an early morning phone call from the receptionist who says, "I'm calling to inform you that the dentist won't be in today and your 2:00 P.M. appointment has been canceled. I'll schedule you for another date. Do you have a preference?"

A preference? What about 3:00 P.M., November 12, 2025?

Dentists are a little peculiar, and I don't understand many of the things they do. Like these:

- They wash their hands more often than a mechanic.
- When reviewing your X-rays they say "Hmmmmmmmmmm" a lot. And that ain't usually in your favor.
- They always hire pretty assistants who hand them things, mix stuff, and watch you spit. She also looks in your mouth while the dentist drills, with a look on her face that says, "My God! What terrible looking teeth!" Her presence in the room is no doubt to keep your mind off whatever the dentist is doing to your molar. It helps, but it ain't always 100 percent effective.

• Dentists always stuff a bale of cotton in each side of your mouth, along with one of those vacuum cleanerlike suction-saliva-remover thingamajigs that makes a sound like bacon frying behind your lower back teeth. Then he tells you not to close your mouth for two hours. Then he washes his hands again and props one arm against the funny looking lamp that hangs above his instrument tray and asks nonchalantly, "Well, tell me, how do you think the Auburn football team will do this year?"

"Igm chtrty frnmkie ucht tdlkgnew adfc gogthimnvhnak," you reply in your best cottonmouth Russian.

"Yeah, I agree," he says. "The quarterback is definitely their main concern."

• Dentists whistle. I'm convinced that whistling is a required course in all dental schools. I also think dentists whistle because with all that cotton and a vacuum cleaner stuffed in your mouth, you can't.

• Dentists scare you to death. Before he starts doing anything with all those tools, he and his pretty assistant pile the tools on that circular tray in front of you, in plain view. Although you are only there for X-rays and a small filling, the man has enough tools on that tray to completely rebuild a diesel engine, including a little round mirror about the size of a penny attached to a five-inch handle. Naturally, when the dentist and his pretty assistant leave the room to check on another patient, or whatever dentists and pretty assistants leave the room to do, you reach for the mirror. You try to sneak a quick peek to see what he's done. Know what happens? You can't see a darn thing for all that cotton, so you try your best to place the little mirror back *exactly* where he left it.

• While in the chair, you listen to piped-in funeral home music, accompanied by the shrill sound of a high-speed drill. The dentist himself provides the lyrics, always the same: "Hmmmmm . . . hmmmmmm . . . uh, hmmmmmmm." Or else he whistles.

• While you sit and squirm in the chair with your mouth wide open like a baby robin, the dentist and his pretty assistant walk around behind you where you can't see them. They mumble inaudible things, rattle instruments, and mix stuff with Super Glue that will eventually make its way into your mouth once the cotton is removed.

● The two most feared and dreaded words in a dentist's vocabulary are *root canal*. It just sounds so deep and expensive. I've heard 'em on several occasions. And answer me this: Why do dentists do most root canals on Friday afternoon and then say as you leave, "Have a nice weekend!" while handing you a prescription for a bushel of Tylenol III tablets? In my case, I gobbled 'em all up Friday night and was standing at the front door of the drugstore early Saturday morning waiting for it to open so I could get a refill. Like I said, I ain't a brave man.

Then there's the story about the fellow who went to the dentist complaining of severe pain in his lower right jaw. After a thorough examination, including the inevitable full-mouth X-rays, the dentist said to him, "I've examined your mouth thoroughly, and I can't find the cause of your complaint. I think it's due to excessive drinking."

"That's all right," said the patient understandingly. "I know how it is. Why don't I just make another appointment and come back when you're sober?"

I'LL NEVER UNDERSTAND
INSURANCE COMPANIES

I don't usually give up easily. It takes a lot to convince me that the ball game is over, that the ship is sinking, or that I'm really overdrawn at the bank. Heck, I was still putting milk and cookies by the fireplace on Christmas Eve when I was forty-two years old. Last year I broke a tooth off my upper plate. Know where it went? Right under my pillow. The fact that I live alone made no difference. I guess the Tooth Fairy was on vacation or had gone to a rock concert, but I will try again.

I have given up completely on one thing, however: insurance companies. I don't understand insurance companies and never have. Although I've been paying health and life premiums for nigh on to forty-five years, for some reason I have never met the deductible. I doubt that Methuselah *ever* met the deductible in all his 900-plus years. But I must admit that my insurance company is very reliable. In all the forty-five years I've been insured with them, they never missed sending me a bill.

If by chance you've ever tried to decipher an "Explanation of Benefits" computer printout, you might just as well be reading a Russian newspaper.

Insurance companies, like lawyers, do not speak or write English. They write and/or speak Insurance. I have no bone to pick with the agents, it's the system and the home office that blow my mind. I'm convinced that the system was conceived by some government agency and programmed by another.

On my desk is a mountain of insurance forms, each plastered with terms that mean absolutely nothing to me. Like these:

- *Major Medical*: I have never been able to determine what is major and what is minor. To me, major is if I have the malady. Minor is if you have it.

- *Applied to the Deductible*: I never have been able to determine how insurance companies come up with how much to apply to the deductible. Judging from my insurance company's reluctance to pay off claims, I think my policy has a one-hundred-dollar debatable.

- *Out of Pocket*: I think I know what it means, but I have always been afraid to ask.

- *Co-insurance*: Does that mean somebody is sharing my insurance with me? If so, why doesn't he spring for half the monthly premium?

- *Uninsured Motorists*: What? I was under the impression that the law required that every motorist be insured.

- *Applicable Discounts*: I have no earthly idea what this means, but I would sure as heck like to get some. Do I write in for 'em, stand in line, or what?

- *Subrogation*: If this means what I think it means, maybe I need to avail myself of the services of a competent attorney. But if his fee is too high, maybe I'll settle for an incompetent one.

- *Death Benefits*: This is an oxymoron if I ever saw one. I guess it means that when I die, I don't have to pay any more premiums.

The main thing I don't understand is the payment of claims provision. If your payment is thirty minutes past due, the insurance company sends you a threatening letter that says in no uncertain terms, "Unless payment is received in this office immediately, we will notify your ex-mother-in-law, your neighbors, your preacher, your librarian, your bank, and your employer that you are a bad credit risk. So there!"

However, submit a claim and see what happens. Nine times out of ten, in about two months you will receive a notice stating, "Send more detailed information in order for us to evaluate your claim. Based on information previously received, we are unable to make a determination."

Always remember this: The fellow who sold you the policy ain't the one who pays the claims.

I submit few claims, but I did submit one on January 7, 1991, on behalf of my mother for reimbursement of prescription drug purchases. Chronologically, this is what happened, and it is documented as fact:

• *January 7*: Claim form submitted for drugs purchased from August through December.

• *February 9*: Letter received from insurance company advising that home office was moving from Atlanta, Georgia, to Illinois, effective February 15. (A toll-free 800 number was furnished).

• *February 28*: I dialed the toll-free 800 number probably twenty times. Busy . . .

• *March 6*: I dialed the 800 number several times, finally got through, and heard this: "All our service representatives are busy. Please hold and one will be with you shortly."

Shortly? I listened to "Autumn Leaves," "Moonlight Serenade," "Stardust," "A String of Pearls," and most of "Theme from *A Summer Place*" before hearing a voice say, "This is Crystal. May I help you?"

"This is Bo. Yes, you may."

I repeated the claim information and asked, "What has happened to the claim?"

I was put on hold again. I wanted very much to hear the rest of "Theme from *A Summer Place*" but was forced to settle for "Mack the Knife" and "King of the Road."

Crystal eventually returned and said, "The computer has no record of your mother's claim. Is she a new policy-holder?"

"Relatively," I said. "About forty-five years, since 1946."

(I could almost hear Crystal say, "Smart ass.")

Standard procedure is, if you can't blame it on the computer, blame it on the move.

"Due to our recent relocation, some of our files are still in Atlanta. Your mother's may still be there. I suggest you call back in about three weeks."

I also had a suggestion. I didn't make it. I'm still surprised at myself that I didn't.

• *April 26*: I called the 800 number again. My luck was getting better. I got an answer on the fifth try. There was no music. I was lucky again. Rock music could have been on, and I could have been placed on hold for hours.

This time I talked to Ginger. I had to repeat everything I'd told Crystal. "I suggest you talk to my supervisor, Catherine Miller," Ginger said.

"Put her on."

"I can't. She's gone to a conference in Chicago and won't be back in the office until April 29th."

• *April 29*: Catherine Miller told me two checks were mailed February 20. I told her they were never received. She said she would stop payment and reissue them, but it would take about three weeks to "cut" them.

"Why is that?" I asked. "It only takes about forty-five seconds when I 'cut' one to pay you."

(I'm pretty sure that then and there I was again labeled a smart ass).

• *June 29*: I called to advise the insurance company that my mother had died that day.

• *July 29*: Two checks arrived, for 17 percent of the amount claimed. There was this note: "Remaining checks being processed." Also, in a separate envelope, this love note: "Premium payment past due since July 1. Unless payment is received on or before August 1, this policy will be canceled effective at 12:01 A.M., August 1, 1991."

Somehow I don't think my mother is really worried about that.

I went back and looked at the notification again that the company headquarters was being moved from Atlanta to Illinois. I couldn't believe the reason: "To better serve you."

INSURANCE INTERPRETERS ARE IN LARGE DEMAND

When I am ignorant on a subject, I will readily admit it. Realizing that I was totally ignorant in the field of insurance, I persuaded a good friend in the business to allow me to accompany him to a four-hour seminar on the subject.

"I just want to listen and learn," I assured him.

The next day we traveled to Cordele, Georgia, where the seminar would be held in the Holiday Inn. I went armed with pad and pencil, prepared to absorb and record the four hours of wisdom that was to make me an insurance whiz kid.

"Participation is important," my friend told me on the way to Cordele. "The more you participate, the more you'll get out of the seminar. I'm registering you as my employee so you'll have the same status as everyone else in attendance."

I did participate, and well, but only during the coffee and doughnut hour prior to the beginning of the seminar. I elaborated on the Persian Gulf War, the baseball season, inflation, the forthcoming 1992 election, the 1988 election, all sorts of pertinent stuff. I was, in all probability, the number one participator in the group.

But then the coffee and doughnut hour ended, and the seminar began. From that point on, I was as mute as a Mafia boss appearing before the Jimmy Hoffa grand jury. The conversation had switched abruptly from the English language to the foreign language of Insurance. Oh, how I longed for an interpreter or an Insurance language dictionary.

There were thirty-seven of us present. The other thirty-six each had at least twenty years' experience in the insurance business. I had at most, eyeing the wall clock at 9:07 A.M., a total of seven minutes.

I listened as the others asked questions, super-intelligent questions. The answers furnished by the instructor had to have come straight from Princeton, Harvard, Yale, or the Brookings Institute. I desperately wanted to participate and came real close once to asking a question, but fortunately I recalled the quotation from some wise philosopher: "It is better to sit there and be thought a fool than to open your mouth and remove all doubt."

My only real contributions to the seminar were turning off the air conditioner once at the request of the instructor, inasmuch as the thermostat was located on the wall adjacent to my right shoulder, and picking up the sheet we all signed to record our presence and walking it to the front of the room.

I really strutted as I walked back to my seat in the back of the room. I could just imagine what the others must have been thinking: *He must own his own agency.* Nonchalant? Poised? Calm? Self-confident? Ha! Perry Como would have looked like a nervous wreck compared to me.

I was asked but one question during the four-hour session and answered it correctly. The question came early, about ten minutes into the seminar, when the instructor asked, "Can everyone in the back of the room hear all right?"

I responded with a loud "Yessir!"

One question; one correct answer. Having scored 100, I sat back, relaxed, listened, and made copious notes for the remainder of the session.

After lunch, my friend and I headed home. I drove and he slept the entire seventy-four miles. As I drove, I thought about all the insurance terms I'd heard that morning. Most were confusing to me, and I began to wonder how an individual might comprehend them upon hearing them for the first time—an individual who was buying his first insurance policy.

This imaginary conversation went through my head:

Picture, if you will, Mr. Jack Lapse, Route 3, Premium, Georgia, who has been caught up in the no-fault law. He is fifty-three years old, married to Jane Coverage, and has never had insurance of any kind on his house or automobile. "I'll take my chances," he would always say.

Lapse is seated at the desk of Slick Talker, owner of the Clippum Quick Insurance Agency in downtown Premium. He has two children—a son, seventeen, and a daughter, nineteen—living at home. The conversation could have gone like this:

"Mornin', Mr. Talker," Lapse says. "Th' lady over at th' tag office told me I can't buy my tag 'til I git some insurance."

"That's right, Lapse. I'll be glad to take care of you," Talker assured him as he reached for pad, pencil, and a rate book. "Hmmmmm . . . let's see now. Have you had any tickets in the past two years?"

"Well . . . yeah. I had two dang good 'uns to a Braves–Pirates game back in May, but it got rained out in th' fourth inning. Doggone good game too, Talker. Them Braves was . . ."

"No, Lapse. I mean speeding tickets."

"Speedin' tickets? Shoot naw! I don't speed."

"Good, very good," said Talker. "Now, as to your limits of liability. Would 10/25 limits be satisfactory?"

"Well, no, not quite. Might be all right for my wife, Talker, but sometimes I drive a little faster than that. Like I said, I don't speed. But I do go more than ten and twenty-five," Lapse advised.

"I see. Well, what about 50/100? That should take care of it, shouldn't it?" Talker asked.

"Ought to, unless my boy is drivin'."

Talker said nothing. He just frowned and gritted his teeth. Lapse lit his pipe.

"All right, 50/100 will take care of your BI and PDL along with BI for UM and we can also add PD for a nominal fee," Talker rattled off in Insuranceese. "You will also want PIP and Medpay along with Comp and Collision with a deductible of a hundred on collision and ACV on the comp, right?"

Lapse took his time and relit his pipe before answering. "Sounds 'bout right to me, Talker."

"Good. Now, now let me see . . . your car falls in Group Three and you and your wife are both Class One . . ."

"Ya got that right, Talker," Lapse said proudly. "Just ask anybody in Premium. They'll tell you that both me an' my ole lady are first class."

Talker didn't bother to reply. He merely shifted in his chair and frowned again as he reached for and opened his little blue rate book. "I see here that you are in Territory Nineteen . . . "

"Nope. You're wrong there, Talker. I'm in the Eighth District, and me and my ole lady both voted for Jack Brookins. He oughta won, too. Doggone good man, that Brookins. Th' way I figure it, he'd a won easy if it hadn't been for . . ."

"Right. OK, Lapse. But I'm talking about Territory Nineteen for rating purposes; not about Mr. Brookins so . . ."

"Whadda ya mean for rating purposes? I rate Brookins right up there with the best of 'em. And let me tell you another thing, young feller . . ." Lapse blurted out as he got up to leave.

"Hold it! Wait a minute, Mr. Lapse. I'm all for Jack Brookins. I voted for him. I was just trying to explain how your car is rated so I can determine the cost of your premium," Talker assured him.

"Well, as long as you put it that way . . ."

Talker turned to his calculator and fingered it like a concert pianist, coming up with a figure of $312.60.

"Sounds a little high to me, Talker," Lapse said, frowning, as he removed his fat wallet from his left rear pants pocket. "Let me think about it f'r a few minutes. Now then, how 'bout givin' me some figures on my house and b'longings, not includin' my bird dogs. You see, Talker, I've 'bout quit huntin' since I got drunk las' year and run my pickup through the gymnasium an' broke my lef' leg an' back. Too bad, too. We was ahead by eight points in the fourth quarter, but they had to call the game off after I knocked the goal down and . . ."

At this point, Talker's mouth got real dry, and he felt a strange emptiness in the pit of his stomach. He merely shook his head as he placed the cover over the calculator and re-placed the pencil in his shirt pocket. He leaned way back in his chair, looked Lapse straight in the eye, and, speaking Insuran-cese, said:

"Well, Mr. Lapse, it appears to me that as far as your Homeowner's policy is concerned, you will need at least an HO-2, and possibly an HO-3, with limited deductions and exclusions, some of which can be handled by endorsements and inasmuch as you are in Fire Class Six you may get a break there. The contents can be handled at ACV and you can schedule your wife's jewelry and your guns. The deductibles can be handled at a flat minimum with an inflation guard for a small 2 percent, quarterly. You are a Code 42, and if you choose to go with an HO-6 Plan for Loss Assessment Coverage or Optional Deductibles with a premium modifica-tion you may qualify for a Preferred Option. Also, you would certainly want to consider the Theft Coverage Extension or Endorsement HO-34 covering other structures. Then you can utilize Basic Forms FR-1, FR-2, and FR-4. Coverage can then be modified and revised to clarify the intent to exclude certain devices covered under FR-8 and FR-10, with certain premium modifications and adjustments, of course. Certain named perils are not identified specifically but can be added by endorsements and . . ."

Talker looked up from his desk just in time to see Lapse putting his hat on his head and his fat wallet back in his pocket as he headed for the door.

"Hey! Mr. Lapse! Wait a minute! I haven't finished explaining your coverage. Where are you going?"

"To see my friend, Jack Brookins, over at his law office and find out if he can get me an interpreter to translate what you're saying," Lapse yelled back over his shoulder as he opened the door on the driver's side to his much-damaged and dented pickup.

COULD EINSTEIN UNDERSTAND
TODAY'S AUTO INSURANCE RATES?

A lbert Einstein was a genius. That's a fact you can take to the bank. He gave the world the $E = MC^2$ Theory of Relativity equation and was awarded the Nobel Prize in Physics for doing so. But even with all his gray matter, I really don't think Professor Einstein could understand today's automobile insurance rates. Anybody who can also deserves a Nobel Prize.

A few thoughts on insurance companies in general:

Where are insurance companies coming from anyway, left field? I received a letter from an insurance company headquartered in Pennsylvania. No warning, no nothing. Just a blunt announcement from Lititz Mutual, Lititz, Pennsylvania, that I should find another insurance company for homeowner's coverage. Bam! Just like that. Here's the letter exactly as I received it:

"We are no longer doing business in the state of Georgia. When your current homeowner's policy expires July 7, it will not be renewed. You should therefore arrange for coverage with another carrier."

Well, so much for the homeowner's coverage. Now a look at automobile insurance rates. What, if anything, will it take to bring them down? I'm convinced it's a hopeless case. Here's why:

• First, we were told that if we required all drivers to have liability (no-fault) insurance, our insurance would go down. We did that.

Mine went up.

• Next, we were told that if we lowered the speed from 65 to 55 miles per hour, our insurance rates would go down. We did that.

Mine went up.

- Also, if we passed tougher DUI laws, our rates would go down. We did that.

Mine went up.

- Next, we were assured that if we raised the drinking age from eighteen to twenty-one, our rates would go down. We did that.

Mine went up.

- Then, we were told that if we passed a mandatory seat-belt law for small children (age five and under), our rates would go down. We did that.

Mine went up.

- Finally, we were told that if we passed a mandatory seat-belt law for everyone, our rates would go down. We did that.

Mine went up.

It appears that the insurance companies, their supposed regulators, and our noble legislators keep socking it to us repeatedly.

Now, a couple of insurance stories:

- An insurance agent who was in the process of selling a health and accident policy to a South Georgia farmer inquired of him if he'd ever suffered any injuries.

"Nope," replied the farmer. "Ain't never had none."

"But I can't help but notice that you limp when you walk," said the agent.

"That's 'cause a mule kicked me in the backside about three weeks ago and a rattlesnake bit me on the leg last Tuesday," the farmer allowed.

"Well, don't you call those accidents?" asked the puzzled agent.

"Nope, I don't," said the farmer.

"Why not?"

"Because," said the farmer, extinguishing a small flame in the fireplace with a squirt of tobacco juice, "the way I figger it, they both done it on purpose."

- Those were memorable days in the early history of our country. Nathan Hale said, "I regret that I have but one life to give for my country." Patrick Henry said, "Give me liberty or give me death." And John Hancock said, "Have I got a policy for you two!"

SECTION THREE

I'LL NEVER UNDERSTAND HOW TO DO SOME THINGS

SOME THINGS ARE JUST HARD TO DO

I have long maintained that there are three things that can't be done: Climb a fence leaning toward you, kiss a girl leaning away from you, and spit into the wind without getting tobacco juice in your face.

There are other things that aren't impossible, just extremely hard to do. Like trying to trim an unruly lock of hair behind your *right* ear with an oversized pair of scissors while looking in the bathroom mirror. I tried it once and almost cut off my *left* ear. My *left* ear!

If you are right-handed, as I am, the mirror immediately reverses that and you become left-handed. Your ears exchange places with each other. So do your eyes and eyebrows. Your nose stays put, but the nostrils swap sides.

After whacking a hunk out of my ear, I managed somehow to stick one blade of the scissors in my right nostril, or was it my left? Only my bathroom mirror knows for sure.

Here are some other things that come to mind that are hard, if not impossible, to do:

- Get in your car when someone has parked too close to it on the driver's side.
- Carry a sofa upstairs (or downstairs) if you're the one walking backward.
- Draw a circle freehand that doesn't resemble an egg.
- Tie a necktie so it comes out even on the first attempt.
- Put the ice trays in the freezer without spilling water.
- Trim the fingernails of your right hand with your left hand if you're right-handed, or vice versa.
- Turn a mattress over alone.
- Change a pillowcase without holding the pillow under your chin.
- Open the door when you're carrying two bags of groceries and a six-pack of Cokes, or whatever.
- Remove anything from your pocket when you have your seat belt fastened.

- Back your car out of your driveway with a utility trailer attached, using only the rear-view mirror for viewing.
- Throw a piece of Scotch tape away with one hand.
- Unscrew a regular screw with a Phillips-head screw-driver.
- Get the color right again on your television set once you've messed it up.
- Remove some foreign object from your eye without having your glasses on, which you had to remove in the first place to get at whatever's in your eye.
- Walk with a full cup of coffee without spilling it.
- Get rid of the toothpick after you've eaten an hors d'oeuvre at a cocktail party or wedding reception.
- Button the collar of a heavily starched shirt.
- Tie a bow tie so that it is straight.
- Go straight home from the office on Friday night.
- Write in a straight line on a blackboard.
- Wrap a package without using Scotch tape.
- Make notes in a telephone book.
- Thread a needle while wearing your first pair of new bifocals.
- Get all the peanut butter out of the jar.
- Make eggs, bacon, grits, and toast come out even.
- Parallel park and, should you succeed, un-parallel park.
- Locate the section of a week-old newspaper that contains the news story you partially read before putting the newspaper aside to go to the golf course.
- Make the gas pump at a self-service gas station stop on even money, say ten dollars, when that is all the money you have with you. The pump will jump to $10.07, at least.
- Remain silent while standing in the "Express, Six Items Or Less, Checkout" line holding but a quart of milk and a loaf of bread while the jerk in front of you has his cart overflowing with seventeen items and the cashier says nothing to him.

In any of these situations, it might help to remember this: No problem is so big or complicated that it cannot be run away from.

THE MOTHER OF
ALL BONEHEAD INVESTMENTS

I made the mother of all bonehead investments in Birmingham, Alabama. I bought an iron and an ironing board. That makes about as much sense as Danielle Steel investing in a creative writing course, Jack Nicklaus investing in golf lessons, or Howard Johnson investing in Holiday Inn stock.

Why did I buy the iron and ironing board? Because at times I do stupid things. My investment cries out for an explanation.

I travel a lot. Therefore, it follows naturally that I do a lot of packing and unpacking. But I'm unable to understand why my clothes aren't as wrinkle-free when I unpack them as they were when I packed them. I'm a pretty darn good packer.

I've reached the point where I no longer use travel bags when traveling by car. I invested in a clothes bar that hangs in the backseat of my car. It has proven to be one of my better investments. I now arrive at my destination as wrinkle-free as an old actress with a new face-lift when I travel by car. Flying is another matter altogether.

When I fly, my clothes get as wrinked as a case of dried prunes. That's because baggage handlers hate rednecks and conspire against me. I'm firmly convinced of that. This is what happens when I fly:

"Hey, Reynaldo! Where ya' want this bulldozer?" asks Juan.

"Just run it up on top of Bo Whaley's luggage!" yells Reynaldo, smirking.

So why buy an iron and an ironing board?

When traveling, I am frequently in contact with the public and appear before them when speaking at luncheons and dinners. I try my best to appear "wrinkle-free," but "wash and wear" won't get it done. An iron will, *if* you know how to use one. Therein lies my problem.

Now hear this. It is the cardinal rule for any man contemplating an attempt at ironing: "Thou shalt not trespass on a woman's turf."

I had seen my mother and grandmother test their irons repeatedly, using the standard and accepted method of testing an iron. It works like this: Saliva is applied to a forefinger which is quickly touched to and removed from a hot iron's surface. If a "*sssstttt*" frying sound is produced by this ritual, the iron is ready for business.

I did as I had seen them do. A sound was produced by the ritual, not a "*sssstttt*" from the hot iron's surface but from my lips. I can't print what I said here, but for several days afterward I was forced to type with nine fingers, my right forefinger having sustained a sizable blister.

What followed was an exercise in frustration and futility:

- I tried to iron a sport shirt, one that has (had) a logo of a polo player on it.
Result: The polo player's stick is gone and his pony cremated.
Lesson: Never leave a hot iron flat down on a polo player and his pony to answer the telephone.
- I then tried my hand at ironing a pair of Levi's. Just above the right rear pocket is (was) a rectangular leather patch with the name *Levi Strauss* etched thereon.
Result: Levi underwent a name change. On my britches his name is now L   uss.
Lesson: Leather scorches quicker than denim.
- Next I tried a dress shirt, blue oxford cloth with button-down collar. I like starched collars, so I saturated it with Niagara spray starch. I let it soak in like the directions said.
Result: I now have one blue oxford cloth shirt with a button-down, galvanized metal collar.
Lesson: "A little dab'll do ya."
- I tackled a pair of pleated pants. I started with four pleats, two on each side of the fly.
Result: I ended up with seven pleats, three on the left of the fly, three on the right of the fly, and one just above the right knee.
Lesson: Never, under any circumstances, attempt to iron pants with pleats.

Among other things, I also learned that no matter where I stood I had to reach over, under, or around the cord; that it is impossible to keep a garment from crawling on an ironing board; that buttons are a nuisance to us ironers; professional ironers in laundries and dry cleaners are ridiculously underpaid, no matter how much they make; and women are grossly underappreciated by husbands and sons.

Ironing is an art. I now pay much closer attention to men's shirts and pants with pleats than I used to before I invested in an iron and ironing board.

A woman is much better at ironing—and most other things around the house—than is a man. So men, say "Thank you" to yours and kiss her tonight when you remove your dirty shirt and wrinkled pants as you get ready for bed.

And if your pants have pleats? Send her flowers tomorrow.

IT WAS SEW SIMPLE WHEN MAMA DID IT

I'm convinced that most men, including this one, are more or less helpless when there's no woman in the house to do the things that women do best, like sewing a button on a shirt. Take it from one who knows. It ain't easy.

I've seen my mother sew on hundreds of shirt buttons. There's an art to it. First, she would roll just enough thread off the spool and either bite it or break it with two fingers. I've tried it. Thread will cut your fingers. I have the scar to verify that. Then she would pop one end of the thread in her mouth and moisten it before twisting it, again with two fingers (thumb and forefinger) to a fine point before threading the needle. Next, she would tilt her head back, twist her lips together tightly, and pop the thread through the eye of the needle on the first try.

She would then stretch the thread to its full length and tie a one-handed knot at the end to keep the end of the thread from following the needle through the hole it would make.

Next, she would push the needle and thread alternatively through the four holes in the button with her thimble-covered right index finger until she was satisfied it was secured. Finally, she would sneak the needle underneath and sew crossways for a few stitches before biting the thread.

She would then check to see if the button was properly aligned with the corresponding buttonhole.

Job completed.

I tried it while getting dressed to go to a wedding. My admiration for button sewers skyrocketed.

I removed the lone clean white shirt from my closet and began buttoning up. I buttoned the right collar button. The left one was missing. Surely, I thought, there is a machine at the laundry that pulls the buttons off my shirts and shoots them through the toes of my socks.

The time was 6:35 P.M. The stores had been closed for thirty-five minutes, and the wedding was at seven o'clock. I had to make a decision. I made a bad one. I would sew a button on my white shirt, but first I had to find one, along with a needle and thread.

I raided an innocent pink shirt and, because I couldn't find my scissors, snipped the bottom button off with a pair of toenail clippers. I prayed that the bride would never know about the toenail clippers. "Something old, something new, something borrowed, something blue" is traditional, but a shirt button removed by toenail clippers ain't part of the tradition.

Next, I had to find the little utility kit that Delta Airlines gave me on a flight from Atlanta to New York. I recalled that included in it was needle and thread. By some miracle, I found it.

Delta was ready, but I wasn't. I had to try to thread the needle while wearing bifocals. I soon began swearing at Delta for having given me an eyeless needle. I saw no hole, and then suddenly I saw two. By some miracle I got the thread through one of them.

Next, the button. It had four holes. I missed several times, pricked my finger twice, dropped the button and watched it disappear under the sofa never to be seen again. I ended up with two little splotches of blood on my collar.

I gave up and went to the wedding decked out in a one-button collar looking like a pigeon with a broken wing. I sat in the back of the church and no one noticed. The reception was another spool of thread.

From the time I signed the bride's book with the traditional feather until I left, I walked around with my head cocked conspicuously to the left, feigning a pulled neck muscle in an attempt to conceal the fact that I was wearing a one-collar-button shirt. I lied repeatedly, telling interested sympathizers that "I must have pulled it while swinging a golf club."

No problem until one observant female approached me from the blind side, touched my collar, and whispered, "Are you aware that there's a button missing from your shirt?"

I never flinched and whispered back, "Oh, thank you! It must have come off when I kissed the bride."

That's when she spotted the two little splotches of dried blood, and asked, "What happened? Did she bite you, too?"

I left it at that.

"MR. FIXIT" AND HIS SKILL SAW

I doubt there are many men alive who don't fancy themselves Mr. Fixits around the house. Just give them a project or two and a few tools, then isolate them in the basement and see what happens. Just don't interfere. Let them saw, drill, and hammer to their hearts' content. They are harmless creatures.

Noel Smith, who lives in Woodstock, Georgia, is such a creature. He fancies himself to be a handyman, a Mr. Fixit, if you will.

Noel would much prefer to putter around in his basement, fixing or breaking things, than to go to a ball game, play golf, or watch television.

One Christmas, Noel's wife, Jamelia, gave her husband a prized and cherished Christmas gift. To Noel it was the perfect gift: a skill saw. When he opened the package, his face brightened. He could hardly wait for a project on which to use it.

(*Note:* It needs to be reported here that Noel and Jamelia have two cats. Please keep that in mind.)

Shortly after Christmas, Noel retreated to his basement, skill saw in hand, to begin what would be the best-kept secret in his neighborhood since the Oak Ridge Atomic Bomb Project in Oak Ridge, Tennessee, some fifty years previously.

He could be heard sawing and hammering nightly until the hour was late. Two months and forty dollars worth of additional tools later, he surfaced with his finished project in hand, anxious to show his handiwork to friends and neighbors, one a most successful and talented building contractor and carpenter.

What was the project of which Noel was so proud? An escape hatch in the door leading from the dining room into the kitchen for his two cats to go through. The space where the door usually hung had been empty for two months.

The unveiling proved somewhat embarrassing for Noel, and

the cats couldn't make heads or tails of his handiwork. In his haste to get started when he placed the door on two work-benches in his basement, Noel constructed the escape hatch six feet from the floor—at the *top* of the door!

The carpenter neighbor, a compassionate soul, came to Noel's rescue. Not only did he repair and close the lofty escape hatch, he also made a new one—at the bottom of the door—in one night.

The talk around Noel's neighborhood was that while his next project with his skill saw is known but to him, he might consider building a doghouse, one big enough for him to get in. After what Noel did to his wife's door, she thinks a doghouse might be a great idea.

Noel's cat-escape-hatch story, which is absolutely true and verified with photographs by his sister who lives in my home-town, reminds me of a somewhat similar story. While it is no doubt fictional, it fits here.

An elderly gentleman was visited one night by an insurance salesman. As they sat in the livingroom and talked in front of a roaring fire in the fireplace, the insurance salesman couldn't help but notice nine holes, graduated in size from large to very small, cut in the *bottom* of the door leading from the livingroom to the bedroom.

"Do you mind my asking what those nine holes in that door are for?" asked the insurance salesman.

"Nope, not at all. I got two cats and seven kittens. They run through them holes when I tell 'em to scat," the old gen-tlemen said.

"But I don't understand," the insurance salesman said. "Why didn't you just make one big hole?"

"Because, son, whenever I say 'Scat!' dadgummit I mean 'Scat!' " he said.

WHEN ALL ELSE FAILS, READ THE DIRECTIONS

It's a fact of life that anything I buy or receive as a gift that has to be assembled, installed, or programmed drives me crazy.

Primarily, that is because I never take the time to read the directions. On the few occasions that I have, I didn't understand them.

The people who write directions are sadists. They sit in hysterics somewhere at their typewriters, overjoyed at the thought that I am *at that very moment* making a vain attempt to assemble, install, or program something for which they wrote the directions. I'm convinced they receive bonuses if they can write directions that nobody can follow.

I'm not the only one in my town stubborn enough not to read and understand directions. A good friend, Ray Prosperi, a former quarterback at the University of Georgia, was recuperating at home from knee surgery when I went to visit him. I took him a few books to help pass the time. I noticed a large box on the floor underneath the window. In bold letters on its side was "VCR."

"Got y'sef a new VCR, Ray?" I asked.

"Oh, no. I've had it for some time now," he replied.

"Can't hook it up, eh?"

"Can't hook it up?" he questioned. "I've only had it four years, and I already know how to set the clock."

Meanwhile, back home in my bedroom is a telephone answering machine. It was a Christmas present from my thoughtful daughter, who may well be in cahoots with the folks who write directions. It is still in its original box, only having been taken out once for a brief attempt to activate it. That was more than three years ago. It has remained in a dormant state since.

The name of the machine is no longer than a telephone call to Japan: "Panasonic Easa-Phone Integrated Telephone System

With Tone Remote Control." It's a super deluxe model. Just look at all the features:

- Tone remote control system
  - OGM recording
  - OGM skip
  - Memory playback
  - Remote turn on/off
  - Room monitor
  - Auto-logic operation
  - Automatic dialing
  - Two-way memo recording
- Switchable tone/pulse
- Tone switching
- Memo dial
- Twelve one-touch dialing systems
  - Redial
  - Incoming message recorder
  - Remote control message receiver

That's an impressive list of things I don't understand. No problem (I thought). I would simply remove the twenty-six-page Operating Instructions booklet and activate the little electronic booger. I should have known better.

Anything requiring twenty-six pages of instructions to educate somebody on how to activate and operate it is automatically trouble.

I spent the better part of two days and one night attempting to get it to work. I finally threw in the towel after following eleven pages and never getting a dial tone. Back in the box it went.

I have a friend who's a professor of electrical engineering and computer technology at Georgia Tech. I decided to wait until the next time he came to town and ask that he have a go at it. If he couldn't activate it, I'd load the box in the trunk of my car and take it to my son Joe's house and have my ten-year-old grandson, Jeremy, do it. It would probably take him ten minutes, maximum. And he wouldn't even read the directions.

I also am the proud owner of a digital clock/radio, also dormant. I bought it back in the days when it was a must that I get up at 6:00 A.M. to do my 7:00 A.M. radio talk show. It worked fine until lightning one night caused a power outage. Notice that we no longer have power shortages. We now have power outages. Either way, when it happens, you ain't got no power. That's when electrical appliances and gadgets, like digital clock/radios, go absolutely bananas. In my case, when the shortage/outage occurred, the dial and the little red light on it blinked like the inside of the command center at NASA. I guess they would still be blinking had I not unplugged the gadget and stored it in the hall closet. Why didn't I reset it, you ask? Simple. As usual, I had thrown the directions away.

I tried but finally gave up on resetting it. I chose to buy a wind-up Big Ben that, when the alarm goes off, sounds like a jail break at Alcatraz, San Quentin, or the Atlanta Federal Penitentiary—or all three at once.

I considered taking the digital clock/radio to Ray Prosperi and ask him to set it for me. I decided against that, however, because I really didn't want to have to wait four years to wake up.

As far as the telephone answering machine is concerned, I actually put it in my car last July to take it to my friend Ed Herrin for his assistance in programming and activating it. That didn't work. Upon arrival at Ed's house, I found him under his carport, up to his skinned elbows and busted knuckles, still trying to assemble his grandson's Christmas scooter. I scratched the idea of even asking, fearing that he might resort to the same language regarding my telephone answering machine that he was leveling at a stubborn and ill-fitting front wheel nut on his grandson's scooter.

I really felt that Ed's efforts to assemble the scooter would be all for naught anyway. After all, at the rate he was going, his little grandson would have his driver's license and a sports car by the time he finished . . . if he finished. There is a difference between finishing and quitting. If I were a betting man, I'd lay ten to one that Ed quits. And I'd lay twenty to one that he will buy the sports car for his grandson. Ed's that kind of a guy.

As I look around my house, I see several other items crying out for attention. They've been crying for several years.

There's the "easy-to-assemble" office chair that I bought on sale in Macon three years ago for my secretary. It is still strewn, partially assembled, in a spare room.

There's the cordless telephone I bought in the hope of gaining a little status. Hah! Its range doesn't extend beyond my front porch.

There's the temperamental microwave oven that will cremate bacon one day but won't thaw chicken the next.

There's the electric blanket that will burn you to a crisp when the temperature is a comfortable 55 degrees. However, when the temperature dips below freezing, it blows a fuse.

I really do have good intentions. I've been meaning to get all these things fixed. I will before Ray Prosperi gets his VCR working and Ed Herrin finishes assembling his grandson's scooter.

Meanwhile, my secretary can continue to sit on a nail keg, and I'll continue to make short-distance telephone calls, eat cremated bacon and frozen chicken, and sleep in a cold bed.

MY KITCHEN SPEAKS
A FOREIGN LANGUAGE

My little house is a simple place, with a couple of bed-rooms, a bathroom, a den, a livingroom, scattered clothes closets, and the monster: the kitchen. My kitchen and I aren't on the same (micro)wave length. I speak what can best be termed regional (southern) English. My kitchen speaks a foreign language, which one I do not know. I only know it doesn't understand me, and I don't understand it. I live alone, so it goes without saying there's no interpreter.

I spent a week in my kitchen one day after receiving an invitation to attend a party at the home of friends. There was a request at the bottom of the invitation—just below the RSVP—that presented a problem for me. The notation sounded sim-ple and would have been for most folks. Not for me. "Please bring a covered dish," it said.

I've received many such invitations with similar notations in the past. No problem. I simply had a restaurant prepare a covered dish, paid for it, and went to the party with covered dish in hand. Or I would go to the grocery store and pick up something at the last minute, cover it, and arrive at the party à la Betty Crocker. But for this party, I was determined to prepare my own covered dish. That presented a problem for this old single man who has extreme difficulty heating hot dogs or making toast without directions.

I had a reason for deciding to prepare my own covered dish. I get sick and tired of other guests whispering behind my back, "Well, I see Bo Whaley has arrived with his usual vienna sausages and saltine crackers." I would remedy that by pre-paring an exotic dish that would knock their hats in the creek.

The day after receiving the invitation, I trucked over to the library and checked out *The Bachelor's Cookbook*. On the way back home with cookbook in hand, the thought flitted through my mind that I might even consider dismissing my personal chefs—Boy-R-Dee, Sara Lee, Colonel Sanders—who have kept me alive for years.

Once home, I eagerly began reading the cookbook. It contained fifty-two menus and, according to the inside cover, "Even the rankest amateur can put together a meal that will draw the astonished applause of friends and family." There was only one thing correct in that statement: rankest amateur. Astonished? Definitely. Applause? No way.

I chose menu twenty-six, an exotic-sounding concoction called Spanakopita (Spinach Pie). That was my first mistake, because I live by the rule, "Never eat anything you can't pronounce."

According to the cookbook, "Every cook has one favorite dish, the one you wheel out for special occasions. It should look sensational when brought to the table, and the first bite should melt in your mouth. During the meal, the dish should be the main topic of conversation." The main topic of conversation? Absolutely right.

The cookbook goes on to say that the first bite should prompt the question, "Mmmmmmm, what's this?" The second bite: "Hey, what *is* this?" By the third bite, people should be asking for a second helping. And by the fourth bite, they should be begging for the recipe. In my case I guess two—the first two—out of four ain't bad.

Here is the recipe for Spanakopita that I tried to follow:

The Staples: Eggs, salt, pepper, oregano, rosemary, garlic, lemons, olive oil, sugar.

The Shopping List: Two pounds of feta cheese, one pound of filo dough, two pounds of spinach, two large onions, one pound of butter.

The Preparation: First, use a pastry brush to spread butter over the thin sheets of dough. Then melt a large chunk of butter—three or four tablespoons—in a frying pan over medium heat. Add an onion, chopped fine, and one clove of garlic, minced. Cook until the onions are softened.

Now for the spinach. Rinse several times in a pot of cold water. Dry it with paper towels, chop it fine, and add it to the onions. Add salt, pepper, a large pinch of oregano, and a large pinch of rosemary.

Separate half a dozen eggs, putting the yolks in one bowl

and the whites in another. Beat the yolks for a few minutes, and blend in one pound of feta cheese, crumbled. Stir in the spinach mixture. Finally, beat the egg whites until they are stiff, and fold them into the rest of the pie filling.

Preheat oven to 350 degrees. Melt half a pound of butter in a saucepan over low heat. Carefully unroll the filo dough, and use a pastry brush to paint the bottom of a rectangular nine-by-thirteen-inch baking dish with melted butter. Lay a single sheet of filo dough over the pan, and brush butter on the dough. Repeat until you have ten sheets of dough. Spoon in spinach mixture and cover with another sheet of dough. Repeat until you have used up the filo. Butter top with pastry brush. Place in oven and bake for 50 minutes.

It all sounds so simple, right? Wrong! Complications immediately.

I had no pastry brush, so I used an old paint brush that had been simmering in turpentine in a coffee can for almost seven years since I painted some concrete blocks. I also had no rosemary, so I called a bachelor friend who is a self-proclaimed expert chef and radio announcer.

"You got rosemary at your house?" I asked.

"Rosemary? Heck no. I don't even know the girl! Why?"

"Because I'm making Spanakopita and . . ." I said.

"Shhhhhhhh! Watch your language, boy! I'm on the air!" he cautioned.

"Well, I need rosemary real bad," I pleaded.

"Oh, yeah? Good luck. How 'bout Margie, Lucy, or Irene? Want their phone numbers?" he asked.

"No, thanks. Got to have rosemary."

My next problem surfaced when I realized I had no paper towels with which to dry the spinach. I used three old newspapers.

I also couldn't find any filo dough. I substituted several slices of white bread, thin sliced. Also, no feta cheese, but the partial can of parmesan left over from a spaghetti dinner a few months back worked fine.

Also, I've never been able to remember the difference between a teaspoon and a tablespoon. Which is larger? I just dropped in three or four of each filled with butter. And inasmuch as I had no "large pinch of oregano," whatever that is, I just pinched rosemary twice and let it go at that, doubled the salt and pepper ingredients, and added half a bottle of Louisiana Hot Sauce on my own, just for good measure.

Finished, I placed the Spanakopita in the oven for the required fifty minutes, or so I thought. But would you believe that my oven conked out in thirteen minutes? No doubt from lack of use.

I removed my Spanakopita, covered the dish with what was left of the newspapers (no aluminum foil or Saran wrap in the house), and took it to the party. I figured that my dish would probably be the star of the buffet table. But just in case, I stuck a couple of cans of vienna sausages and a box of saltines in my pockets—for Rosemary, if she happened to be there.

As predicted in the cookbook, the first bite produced a chorus of "What's this?" The second bite—right on cue— produced a second chorus of "What *is* this?"

I said nothing, but I can tell you that the vienna sausages and saltines were delicious.

Rosemary? She never showed up. I figured she was probably at my radio announcer friend's house.

SECTION FOUR

WORDS ARE FOR COMMUNICATIN'

DO YOU EVER TAKE THE TIME TO LOOK IT UP?

Writers are a peculiar breed. I admit that. For many years I have been reading and writing, and in the process I have passed over or ignored words and phrases completely foreign to me. When I encountered them, I merely kept on reading or writing, never bothering to stop and take the time to look them up in my dictionary.

My good friend, Paul Watson, Jr., reads three newspapers while eating breakfast every morning in his favorite haunt, McDonald's in Dublin, Georgia. While Paul doesn't smoke cigarettes, his shirt pocket is never empty. He keeps a small dictionary in it. When he comes across an unfamiliar word, he stops, removes his little dictionary, and looks it up. He's been doing it for as long as I've known him, about forty years. And the guy has one heck of a vocabulary.

I vowed several years ago that I would emulate Paul, promising myself repeatedly that I would replace my cigarette pack with a dictionary. I haven't done it yet, but I haven't given up, either.

I did take the time recently to open my office dictionary and determine the real meaning of a few words that have been mysteries to me since childhood. Actually it was quite revealing to know for the first time the meanings of these words that I've been reading:

- *Ad hoc*: Since I was old enough to hold a newspaper, I've read about committees, legislative committees, congressional committees, church committees, school committees, civic club committees, and the like. I've also served on several committees. Many times I've read about *ad hoc* committees, but I've never had the faintest idea what one was. I only knew that it sounded like something that one would see on a public restroom wall, and I shouldn't bandy it about in mixed company. Also, it sounds like what you do before you spit on the ground.

I looked it up. "An *ad hoc* committee is a committee estab-lished for the particular end or case at hand without consideration of wider application." In plain language, it is to examine one specifically defined area and then quit. Finis. Period. The end. No more. Stop. Adjourn. Halt. Terminate. Go no further.

Example: "The president has appointed an *ad hoc* committee to study night life of selected senators and representatives." (And that's something that shouldn't be bandied about in mixed company.)

• *Sic*: Although I've been confronted by this little booger many times, I never understood its meaning until recently. I just always more or less considered *sic* to be part of a com-mand to prompt one dog to attack another. Not true at all, I learned.

Sic simply means, "intentionally so written and used after a word or passage to indicate that it is intended exactly as printed, or to indicate that it exactly reproduces an original."

Example: "She's the type of woman that the more you see less of her the better more you don't like her" (*sic*).

Example: "If you don't get out of here and leave me alone, I'll find somebody who can" (*sic*).

Example: "I knewed I knowed you when I seen you caming so I flung up my hand and wove to you but you don't know who I are, had you?" (*sic*).

• *Sans*: I plead ignorance to *sans*. Admittedly, I thought it was merely the first four letters in the brand name of a popular brand of men's slacks or the first name of a Las Vegas casino. It is neither.

Sans is afforded a one-word definition by Mr. Webster, who says it means "without."

Example: Not everybody is familar with the definition of the little word as evidenced by this exchange that reportedly took place between a coffee shop waitress and a customer:

"I'd like a cup of coffee *sans* cream, please," the customer said.

"Ain't got no cream," she said. "You'll have to take it *sans* milk."

"Nope, I don't drink my coffee *sans* milk. I drink my coffee *sans* cream," he said indignantly and got up and walked out *sans* coffee of any kind.

- *Et cetera* or *etc*: It is defined as "a number of additional persons or things, additional items; odds and ends." For fear that you might have already judged me totally ignorant, let me hasten to inform you that I learned the meaning of *etc.* many years ago while an employee of the federal government, the originator of the office memorandum. I learned this about *etc.:* When you receive a government memorandum bearing a hand-scribbled note at the end, in the margin, ending with *etc.*, it simply means, "I don't know either, so I'm passing it along for someone else to fix responsibility."

Let me hasten to add that in the federal government there are lots of odds and ends, some elected, some not.

- *Quasi*: This one baffled me for years before I took the time to look it up. I always wondered, could it be like, you know, "Quasi, man!" spoken by a tongue-tied hippie? Or maybe a four-year-old at the state fair begging his mama to let him go inside the "Quasi house?" I think not.

A quick check with Webster provided this definition: "In some sense or degree. Having some resemblance, usually by possession of certain attributes."

For the most part, I've read about quasi having to do with quasi-judicial, which means "having a partly judicial character by possession of the right to hold hearings on and conduct investigations into disputed claims and alleged infractions of rules and regulations and to make decisions in the general matter of courts."

Based on the above definition, there is no doubt in my mind that some committees, like the Senate Judiciary Committee, are indeed quasi. In fact, the Senate Judiciary Committee is quasi as a lunatic, or fourteen lunatics.

Now, I must take leave of this subject. I have a most interesting book that I'm just dying to get into, *sans* interruption, etc. Have to keep abreast of things by reading intellectual books, you know, and I plan to read my new book *ad infinitum.*

WHAT EVER HAPPENED
TO THE OLD WORDS?

I doubt my grandfather would recognize the English language if he were alive today. It is a far cry from the language he knew and employed prior to his death in 1944. Somewhere along the line many words have changed drastically to the point of having become obsolete or in some cases extinct.

If my grandfather characterized a friend as not feeling well, he would use the word *puny*, which simply meant not "up to snuff." On the other hand, if the friend was indeed ill and had been to see a doctor, he would use the word *peekid*, instead of puny, which meant that the friend had changed color and needed medicine.

Bilious was a term used almost exclusively by the affluent, which meant that an individual was either puny or peekid, but nobody knew exactly what was wrong with him.

Also, back then people got "stove up" a lot. It was sort of a cover-everything term. And some people were just "under the weather," which covered everything from a chest cold to being kicked by a mule.

Not only have the words used back then to describe one's physical condition changed, our entire vocabulary has undergone a transplant.

Here are examples of the way it used to be, as opposed to the way it is now:

Soda crackers: Saltines
Dinner: Lunch
Supper: Dinner
Kodak: Camera
Constipation: Irregularity
Dope fiend: Drug abuser
Overalls: Jumpsuit
Parlor: Florida room

Barber: Stylist
Spyglasses: Binoculars
Victrola: Tape deck
Poor: Underprivileged
Fat: Full-figured
Crazy: Emotionally disturbed
Weenie: Frankfurter
Queer: Gay

False teeth: Dentures
Little bitty: Mini
Ice box: Refrigerator
Snacks: Hors d'oeuvres
Gearshift: Straight stick
Hubcaps: Wheel covers
Wheel: Bicycle
Bad cold: Virus
Linoleum: Floor covering
Reform school: Youthful
  offender rehabilitation
  facility
Drunk: Alcohol abuser
Shackin' up: Cohabitating
Picture show: Theater
Den: Great room
Sissy: Effeminate
Convict: Inmate
Settee: Sofa
Welfare: Department of Family
  and Children's Services
Prison: Correctional facility
County jail: County law
  enforcement center
Rotten kid: Juvenile delinquent
Bum: Homeless
Sanforized: Preshrunk
Flirting: Harassing
Fired: Involuntarily separated
State Prison Department:
  Department of Offender
  Rehabilitation
Old Age Pension: Social
  Security
Poorhouse: Retirement Facility

Old man (old woman): Senior
  citizen
Automobile gas tank nozzle: Fuel
  access spout
Dog pound: Animal shelter
Dog catcher: Animal control
  officer
Schoolhouse: Comprehensive
  Learning Facility
Janitor: Supervisor of
  custodial services
Catalog: Brochure
House trailer: Mobile home
Grocery store: Supermarket
Church: Family Christian
  Center
Side road: Access road
Brown: Earth tones
Personality: Charisma
He-man: Macho man
Dirty pictures: Porn
Not-quite-so-dirty pictures: Soft
  porn
Used car: Preowned
Deodorant: Antiperspirant
War Department: Department
  of Defense
Xylophone: Vibes
Chain gang: Work detail
Personnel manager: Director of
  Human Resources

And whatever happened to
davenports and chifforobes?

ENGLISH CAN BE VERY CONFUSING

The ripe old age of sixty-three is probably a little late in life to come up with a pen pal, but that's what I've done. And Henry Bowden's a good one, too.

Henry is a lifelong resident of Atlanta, Georgia, and one of that city's outstanding attorneys. He has been for fifty-two years.

I met Henry through the wonderful world of rednecks in 1990, after he received two of my books as gifts. He wrote me a nice, complimentary letter, and I sent him the other six books. Several months later we had lunch together in Atlanta. Delightful.

The man loves to write for his own enjoyment, and periodically he sends me samplings. A good writer, he sticks to basics. For a man who recently turned eighty-one, he's as frisky as a young colt.

Here are two examples of why it is always a treat for me to hear from Henry Bowden:

Odd expressions: Often I have wondered about the origins and meanings of some expressions used frequently in conversation. Some that readily come to mind are:

- "She could talk the horns off a brass monkey."
- "She can't hold a candle to him."
- "That's one for the birds."
- "Now that's a real lulu."
- "He can't come to the phone right now. He's all tied up."
- "Get a hump on."
- "Quiet as a church mouse."
- "Up in arms."
- "A brickbat."
- "Let me put in my two-cents' worth."
- "He's falling all over himself."
- "Sound as a dollar."
- "He was beside himself."

Now then, the few monkeys I've seen have no horns, and they certainly weren't brass. When I think of someone being tied up, I picture a fellow with ropes all around him tied securely, making him immobile. I know what a brick is, also a bat; but I never have seen a brickbat. In recent days the dollar hasn't been the height of solidarity by any stretch of the imagination. With inflation, the expression about putting in two-cents' worth has surely risen to a quarter. And how, pray tell, can a man fall all over himself or sit beside himself? Impossible, I say.

Foreign language and ours. It seems to me that it would be very hard to learn to speak Russian, Chinese, Japanese, and other foreign languages. But English seems so simple to me. Is it?

Take the word *date*. In English it may mean a fruit, the day of the year, month, and week, or an engagement that a male and a female have for companionship. Similarly, the word *strike* may mean to hit something, a certain type of pitch in baseball, a dissatisfied group of workers quitting in protest, a perfect achievement in bowling, finding oil when drilling, or mining.

Take the word *mean*, which may indicate a bad personality or attitude. It may also indicate an intention but could well indicate the average temperature.

The word *well* is fascinating. It may indicate that you are not sick, or it may mean a hole in the ground with water at the bottom. I can imagine a foreigner saying to a fellow countryman, "I asked him how he was feeling, and he replied that he felt like a hole in the ground with water at the bottom."

Conclusion: Foreigners might experience just as much difficulty with our language as we do with theirs. Tolerance, on both sides, is dictated here.

REFLECTIONS OF A CHRONIC NOSTALGIA BUFF

I guess every small town in America has its own homespun philosophers and the little country stores where they spin their yarns and advance their theories and ideas.

I remember fondly some of the ones I knew as a boy growing up in south Georgia, and I spent many happy days sitting in my grandfather's country store listening. His town of Powelton boasted a population of around 135, among them Lunce Brake, Alex Burnley, George Rocker, and Sam Chapman. They all played checkers at Wes Whaley's store, with bottle caps, and waxed philosophic about everything from Franklin D. Roosevelt to Gene Talmadge to government in general. I never knew, and still don't know, what any of them did for a living. I can't recall any of them ever working.

In Alma there was Holstein Lee's Drug Store, on the corner, naturally. The philosopher in residence was "Shack" Roberts. I never knew his first name. Neither am I able to associate any type employment with him. I just recall that "Shack" spent most of his time at Holstein Lee's Drug Store, was a good friend of my father's, weighed well over 350 pounds, drank Cokes all day long, smoked Camel cigarettes, and drove a little Ford roadster with a rumble seat.

In Oglethorpe there was Dan Kleckley's Grocery, next to the courthouse. The resident philosopher there was Col. Jarred J. Bull, the long-haired lawyer written about earlier who rolled cigarettes with one hand.

In Lumpkin the gathering place was the Singer Company. In Metter the gathering spot was Franklin Chevrolet. In Reynolds it was Goddard's General Store and Whatley's Drug Store.

I could go on and on about such places and the gems of wisdom that came from them. Gems like these:

- "Never trust a man who don't eat grits."
- "Never buy anything that has to be assembled."

Never is the key word and here are a few more that come to mind. They're definitely taboo in the eyes of the country store philosophers.

- "Never shake hands with a policeman while wearing brass knuckles."
- "Never wear a coonskin cap to a Moose or Elks club."
- "Never dance while wearing golf shoes."
- "Never buy instant coffee on the lay-away plan."
- "Never buy anything that includes a sheet of paper that says 'Just Follow These Simple Instructions'."
- "Never wear flip-flops to a wedding."
- "Never pick up a porcupine with your bare hands."
- "Never order chitlins at the Waldorf Astoria, or quiche at Buster's Barbecue and Transmission Repair Shop."
- "Never make an ugly face at a Doberman."
- "Never attempt to play the trumpet while chewing bubble gum."
- "Never try to eat Georgia grits with Chinese chopsticks."
- "Never drink hot tea or iced coffee. The good Lord never intended it that way."
- "Never let anybody from nowhere make fun of the way you talk."
- "Never loan your knife, shotgun, or pickup to nobody."
- "Never turn your back on any man wearing an earring."
- "Never run when you can walk."
- "Never walk when you can ride."
- "Never stand up when you can sit down."
- "Never sit down when you can lie down."
- "Never wear anything chartreuse or lavender."
- "Never wear lace-up boots when you have athlete's foot."
- "Never love a stranger. Be sure and get the name first."
- "Never stick chewing gum behind your ear."
- "Never wear knickers in public . . . or anywhere else."

- "Never criticize the farmer while your mouth is full of food."
- "Never strike a match to check the contents of your gas tank."
- "Never go to the bank to make a deposit while wearing a ski mask."
- "Never play poker with a man who wears long sleeves."
- "Never take a mother's love for granted."

SHHHHHH! LISTEN AND LEARN

There's a lot to be said for doing more listening than talking. Spies know this. So do psychiatrists, telephone operators, counselors, and eavesdroppers. One United States Senator knew this. So did a famous baseball player.

It was Everett Dirksen, the golden-voiced senator from Illinois, who said, "You ain't learning nothing when you're talking; you only learn when you're listening." And Yogi Berra, longtime catcher for the New York Yankees, echoed the senator's opinion when he said, "You can hear a lot by just listening."

Here are some things overheard by just listening:

- Driving instructor overheard telling confused student: "Lady, those little objects you keep complaining about that you say keep you from concentrating are the accelerator and the brake pedals."
- Door-to-door salesman to housewife: "Now, let me show you a little item your neighbors said you couldn't afford."
- One rat in a laboratory cage to another: "I've finally got Dr. Baskin conditioned. Now every time I press the little bar and stand on my head, he gives me a piece of cheese."
- Mother, tucking youngster into bed: "Honey, if you want anything at all during the night, just call Mommy—and she'll send Daddy in."
- Little boy to his friend upon leaving a movie: "I like television better. It's not so far to the bathroom."
- Fight manager to his new heavyweight: "Don't be so terrified. Just remember. If he was any good, he wouldn't be fighting you."
- In a small town barber shop: "Just give me a shave. I haven't got the time to listen to a haircut."
- Young woman in telephone booth to impatient man waiting to replace her: "This won't take much longer. I just want to hang up on him."

- Sweet little old lady at an airline ticket counter in the Dallas/Fort Worth airport: "And how long a hangover will I have in Atlanta?"

- In a locker room at the golf course: "The only way my kids know I'm home from the office is if I walk in front of the television set."

- At the Stork Club: "My fiancé likes the same thing I do, only he likes to save it and I like to spend it."

- Patron to a clerk in a branch post office: "This package contains a *very* fragile and expensive vase, so please throw it underhand."

- At a new shopping center in Atlanta: "What do you mean you don't sell used transmissions? What kind of drugstore is this, anyhow?"

- Man with a terrible hangover hollering at his cat: "Confound it! Stop stamping your feet all over that carpet."

- Eight-year-old to his favorite teacher: "Pop came in very late last night and ran into the garage door. Lucky thing for him he didn't have the car."

- In a crowded department store elevator: "Take your hands off me this minute! No, not you. *You!*"

- In the assembly room of a large manufacturer: "I'm truly sorry, Max, but if I let you take off two hours for lunch today, I'd have to do the same thing for every other technician whose wife gave birth to quintuplets."

ASK A STUPID QUESTION
AND YOU GET A STUPID ANSWER

A t one time or other, all of us have no doubt been subjected to stupid questions. I'm going to list a few of them, along with suggested replies that may come in handy the next time somebody tosses one your way. Just clip and save, or make a copy and tuck it away in your wallet or handbag for ready reference . . . just in case.

Setting the scene: You are just finishing dinner with a few friends at the local restaurant. After placing your napkin on the table and your knife and fork on an empty plate, you reach for your check and say to no one in particular, "Well, I'll see you folks later. I'm goin' to th' house and watch the Braves take on the Dodgers."

Stupid question: "Oh, is the game on television?"

Suggested reply: "No, but I have this ultrapowerful telescope mounted on top of my house, so I just aim it in the direction of Atlanta, watch the game through my telescope, and listen to the play-by-play on my radio."

Setting the scene: You are getting into your automobile in the mall parking lot when a long-time friend calls out to you from his pickup in the next lane, "Hey! Where ya' goin' in such a hurry?"

"I'm goin' to see Walter Bass," you reply. "He had a brain operation yesterday morning."

Stupid question: "Is he in the hospital?"

Suggested reply: "Oh, no. He's at home. He didn' feel up to going to th' hospital, so the surgeon performed the operation on a picnic table in Walter's backyard."

Setting the scene: You pull into a gasoline station about a six-pack north of Broxton, Georgia, and maneuver your car back and forth several times until you get the opening to the gas tank lined up just right for the unleaded pump. It's not a self-service gasoline station. The attendant finally shuffles out to your car and pops the question to you.

Stupid question: "Didja' want some gas?"

Suggested reply: "No, not really. You see, I have this wisdom tooth that has been killing me for the last 200 miles, and I was just wondering if you might take a look at it and give me your opinion as to what I should do about it."

Setting the scene: It's a bright spring day, and you pull up in front of a bait and tackle shop. Four fishing poles are sticking out of the back of your pickup truck. You tell the owner of the shop that you'd like to buy one hundred crickets, a quart of Louisiana pinks, and a six-pack of Bud Light.

Stupid question: "Plannin' to do a little fishin', eh?"

Suggested reply: "No, I'm not. You see, it's like this. I hate crickets and worms, so I go down to the river about twice a week and drown 'em, one at a time. Been doin' it f'r years, and eventually I plan to drown 'em all. I don't even try to catch no fish, but occasionally I am able to talk a few into surrendering."

Setting the scene: After picking up the morning mail, you leave the post office and walk toward your car. En route, you meet a friend you haven't seen in weeks. The two of you shake hands, and he says, "Where in the world have you been? I haven't seen you since I don't know when."

"I've been in the hospital," you say. "Just got out yesterday."

Stupid question: "Oh, were you sick?"

Suggested reply: "Who, me sick? Heavens no! I just felt like taking some time off, so I checked into the hospital for several days. You know, watch a little television and catch up on my reading. Besides, I love the food."

Setting the scene: You are leaving the library with an armload of books up to your chin. As you exit the front door, you meet a stranger coming toward you.

Stupid question: "Looks like you're getting all set to do quite a bit of readin', eh?"

Suggested response: "No, not really. Actually, I have this kitchen table that's not level. The thing bugs me to death, so every two weeks I come here to the library and check out a few books to put under the legs in order to level it up. Over the years, I've determined just how many inches of books I need to get the job done. It takes exactly fourteen inches."

Setting the scene: You are in a card shop browsing in the "new baby" section. You find just *the* card and walk to the cashier, who remarks what a sweet card you have selected.

"Thank you," you say. "It's for Denise Harmon. Her baby is due next week and . . ."

Stupid question: "Denise? Is she pregnant?"

Suggested response: "Is there any other way?"

PLAYING AROUND WITH OXYMORONS

I was introduced to a new word—*oxymoron*—while participating in a seminar at South Georgia College in Douglas, Georgia. The coordinator of continuing education introduced it to me, giving me two examples: "Parting is such sweet sorrow," from Shakespeare's *Romeo and Juliet*, and the word *bittersweet*, an oxymoron unto itself.

An oxymoron is a combination of contradictory or incongruous words, the dictionary tells me. I became interested and took out pad and paper. I'm sure you can add many to the list, but these oxymorons came to mind over a couple of days:

- Jumbo shrimp
- Full-time hobby
- Closet exhibitionist
- Studied indifference
- Minor surgery
- Old news
- Only choice
- Serious humor
- Critical acclaim
- Modern history
- Safe sex
- Nondairy creamer
- Small change
- Barely dressed
- Plastic glasses
- Down escalator
- Pretty ugly
- Eloquent silence
- Uncommonly typical
- Airline schedule
- Family vacation
- Military intelligence
- Congressional ethics
- Standard deviation
- Flat curves
- Extensive briefing
- Ill health
- Civil War
- Unbiased opinion
- False pearls
- Even odds
- Willing slave
- Round numbers
- Moral Majority
- Cold as hell
- Awfully good
- Constant change
- Routine emergency

CONFESSIONS OF A QUIP CLIPPER

I plead guilty. I'm a quip clipper. I've been clipping them for many years. I have boxes and boxes filled with them.

I'm convinced that somewhere there is a Quip Club. The only requirement for membership is the ability to quote quips. Meetings are held weekly, with no set program or format. The quip clippers simply sit in rocking chairs arranged in a semicircle and take turns quoting clipped quips.

Were I a member—with my own rocking chair—here are some of the quips I'd quote when it came my turn:

- My favorite book title: *How to Jump-Start Your Husband.*
- Elementary school student to mother: "Talk about a bad day! We had a math test, a spelling test, and broccoli casserole for lunch, and it rained during recess."
- Husband to marriage counselor: "Of course we share the household chores—she cooks and I eat."
- Classified ad: "Wanted: Singer for new rock band. Must be male or female."
- "Where else but in Washington, D.C., would they call the department in charge of everything outdoors the Department of the Interior?"
- "How come the windshield wiper always works better on the passenger's side?"
- "If swimming is so good for your figure, why do whales look the way they do?"
- A rare book collector met a man who said he'd just thrown away an old Bible that had been packed away for generations.

"Somebody named Guten-something-or-other had printed it," the man explained.

"Not Gutenberg!" gasped the book collector.

"Yeah, that's it, Gutenberg."

"Man, you've thrown away one of the most famous books ever printed! A copy recently sold at auction for $4 million!"

The man, still unmoved, remarked, "Well, my copy probably wouldn't have brought a dime."

"Why not?"

"Because some guy named Martin Luther scribbled notes all in it."

- Teenager to librarian: "I need a copy of a play by Shakespeare."

"Which one?" the librarian asked.

Frowning in concentration, the teenager finally replied, "William."

- Young boy to playmate at door: "Sorry, but I can't come out and play. I'm gonna be tied up for a little while. I promised my folks I'd show them how the VCR works—again."

- Wife to husband: "What do you like most about me, my natural beauty, my gorgeous body, or my superior intelligence?"

Husband: "Your sense of humor."

- Classified ad: "For sale cheap. Almost new VCR. Never learned how to hook it up."

- Husband answering phone late at night: "How the heck would I know? Call the weather bureau," and hung up.

Voluptuous wife: "Who was that, dear?"

Husband: "Beats me. Some guy wanted to know if the coast was clear."

- Divorced man, age fifty-five, to beautiful twenty-two-year-old girl in singles bar: "Where have you been all my life, baby?"

"Teething," she replied.

- Man to bartender: "Guess what? I just walked out on my wife."

Bartender: "Oh, yeah? How'd she take it?"

Man: "It's absolutely amazing. You live with somebody for twenty-two years but really never know them. I had no idea she could turn cartwheels, do somersaults, and sing at the same time."

- A man went to see the movie *Lassie, Come Home* and was amazed to see a matronly woman with a big collie sitting in front of him. He was even more amazed by the fact that the dog always laughed and cried in the right places.

On the way out of the theater, he approached the woman and said, "Excuse me, but I think it's astounding that your dog enjoyed the movie so much."

"Frankly, I'm quite surprised myself," she replied. "He hated the book."

NEVER TAKE WHAT YOU SEE
FOR GRANTED

Magicians are great illusionists. They have the unique ability to do one thing and make it look completely different. Flim-flam artists can do the same thing and leave you with a handkerchief full of newspaper cuttings you'd swear was the money—your money—you saw him put in the handkerchief before handing it to you for safekeeping until he got back from wherever.

Con artists do it with slick talk and quick hands. Card sharks do it with playing cards. Circus acrobats? Their stunts can be deceiving as well, as this little story points out.

Two vagrants, R. J. and Roy Lee, both pretty much into the sauce, stopped at a farmhouse near Sarasota, Florida, the winter home of Ringling Brothers Circus, and knocked on the back door. It was a cold and dreary February day.

Shortly, the lady of the house appeared and asked of them why they were there.

"We was just wonderin', ma'am, if you got any work we could do for you to make a little money to buy somethin' to eat?" R. J. asked.

"We been outta work for a spell and we're hungry," Roy Lee added.

The woman looked them over closely before saying anything. She considered their dirty clothes, rumpled hair, and the smell of alcohol—very noticeable. Finally, she spoke: "Well, do you see that pile of stove wood over there by the chicken house?"

Both men looked, and R. J. confirmed that he saw it. "Yessum, I see it."

"All right, if you're really hungry and want to split the wood, I'll cook you a good dinner. Pork chops, vegetables,

homemade biscuits, and chocolate cake for dessert," she of-
fered. "Also, I have a brand new ax that has never been used.
I just bought it last week."

It was agreed that the two of them would split the stove
wood. The lady handed Roy Lee the ax and both he and R. J.
shuffled off slowly toward the woodpile.

The lady began to cook and through the kitchen window
watched R. J. and Roy Lee reluctantly taking turns splitting the
stove wood. They also took turns with the small bottle of
liquid heat that R. J. kept in his back pocket. She smiled. Then
the telephone rang.

The caller was a lady missionary scheduled to speak at a
meeting of the farm wife's church study group to be held that
very afternoon at 3:00 P.M. in her home. The missionary's
voice was barely audible. She explained that she was calling to
report that she had a bad case of laryngitis, and it would be
impossible for her to speak to the study group that afternoon.

"Oh, my goodness!" exclaimed the farm wife. "What in the
world will I do about a program?"

After appropriate apologies, the missionary hung up, leaving the farm wife in a dilemma. But then, as luck would have
it, or so she thought, fate stepped in.

She looked out the kitchen window to check on the two
wood splitters. At that moment she saw Roy Lee drop the ax,
do two back flips, grab his left foot with both hands, hop on
one foot, jump an eight-foot fence, climb up on a tractor,
shimmy up on top of the chicken house, let out a blood-
curdling Tarzan yell, and plunge headlong into a haystack—
never releasing his grip on his left foot with his hands.

"Amazing! Absolutely amazing!" the farm wife said out
loud, subconsciously thinking "circus acrobat" and her
women's study club meeting.

She ran to the back door, opened it, and yelled to R. J., who
was standing nonchalantly on top of the woodpile leaning on
the ax while watching Roy Lee go through his routine.

"Do you think your friend would agree to do what he just
did again this afternoon at three o'clock for a hundred dollars?" she asked in desperation.

"Don't know, ma'am," R. J. replied. "Ya want me to ask
him?"

"Oh, yes! Please do!"

"All right, I'll ask him," R. J. said. "Hey! Roy Lee!"

"Yeah, what is it, man?" Roy Lee moaned from the haystack.

"You wanna cut off another toe for a hundred dollars?"

TRIVIA CONTEST WAS A MISMATCH

Every now and then I become engaged in a classic mismatch. It happened in Atlanta, Georgia, while I was having dinner with my buddy Ludlow Porch and his wife, Diane.

While enjoying the soup and waiting for the steaks, I made the mistake of challenging Ludlow to a trivia match. I should have known better. That's like challenging Wyatt Earp to a gunfight or Edwin C. Newman to a game of Scrabble. Ludlow is one of five recognized trivia experts in the world, so designated by *Sports Illustrated* magazine.

The subject was double nicknames. I started it. The outcome was never in doubt.

There are people with double nicknames for which they are better known than their real names. Here are four examples:

"Two-Ton Tony" (Galento)
"Diamond Jim" (Brady)
"Charlie O." (Finley)
"Neon Deion" (Sanders)

Get the idea? OK, here are fifty more that date from the Great Depression to the present. Try your hand and see how many you can name, then check the answers below:

1. "Slingin' Sammy"
2. "Light Horse Harry"
3. "Vinegar Bend"
4. "Smilin' Jack"
5. "Gorgeous George"
6. "Dangerous Dan"
7. "Tricky Dick"
8. "Dandy Don"
9. "Dirty Harry"
10. "Dugout Doug"
11. "Big Train"
12. "Scarface Al"
13. "Sad Sam"
14. "Shoeless Joe"
15. "Crazy Legs"
16. "Charmin' Harmon"
17. "Joltin' Joe"
18. "Pretty Boy"
19. "Broadway Joe"
20. "Flatfoot Frankie"

21. "Stan the Man"
22. "Slammin' Sammy"
23. "Choo-Choo"
24. "Little Richard"
25. "Papa Bear"
26. "Splendid Splinter"
27. "Rapid Robert"
28. "Easy Ed"
29. "Blood and Guts"
30. "Buffalo Bill"
31. "Calamity Jane"
32. "Wild Bill"
33. "Push 'em up Tony"
34. "Galloping Ghost"
35. "Tiny Tim"
36. "Vinegar Joe"
37. "Meat Cleaver"
38. "The Refrigerator"
39. "Billy the Kid"
40. "The Dutchman"
41. "Squirmin' Herman"
42. "Big O."
43. "Black Jack"
44. "Mr. October"
45. "The Desert Fox"
46. "Man Mountain"
47. "Little John"
48. "Little Orphan Annie"
49. "The Hammer"
50. "Lonesome George"

I hope you fared better than I did. To check your answers, turn the page.

Answers to Trivia Quiz

1. Baugh	26. Williams
2. Lee	27. Feller
3. Mizell	28. McAuley
4. Martin	29. Patton
5. Wagner	30. Cody
6. McGrew	31. Burke
7. Nixon	32. Hickock
8. Meredith	33. Lazerri
9. Callahan	34. Grange
10. MacArthur	35. Khaury
11. Johnson	36. Stillwell
12. Capone	37. Weaver
13. Jones	38. Perry
14. Jackson	39. Boney
15. Hirsch	40. Van Brocklin
16. Wages	41. Wiedemeyer
17. DiMaggio	42. Robertson
18. Floyd	43. Pershing
19. Namath	44. Jackson
20. Sinkwich	45. Rommel
21. Musial	46. Dean
22. Snead	47. Little
23. Justice	48. Silo
24. Penniman	49. Aaron
25. Halas	50. Gobel

YOU CAN LEARN A LOT FROM READING COOKBOOKS

The next time you're snowed in in Buffalo or find yourself with nothing to read on a rainy night in Georgia, take one of your cookbooks down off the shelf and settle down for the night with it. I've done that. The experience proved very enlightening.

The more names of recipes I read, the more I realized how familiar they were. Soon I concluded that most are named after people I know or have known. Like these:

- *Beef Stroganoff*: Bouncer at Mel's Juke, home base of Robbie Nell Bell, from Alma (Robbie Nail Bail, fum Almer), located about a six-pack north of Broxton on U.S. 441 in South Georgia.
- *Fruit Medley*: Waiter at the Lavender Orchid Restaurant, Atlanta, Georgia.
- *Apple Pan Dowdy*: Head cheerleader at her high school and candy striper at a hospital in Chattanooga, Tennessee. Also a straight A student and president of the Beta Club.
- *Waldorf Salad*: Waldorf, twenty-seven and single, is the only child of Margarita and Chivas Salad. He is heir-apparent to the Salad family fortune, rumored to be larger than the national debt. Spends his time yachting at Kennebunkport in summer and skiing at Aspen and Vail in winter. Can't make change for a dollar but is most adept at signing credit cards. Drives a Porsche and drinks Perrier and Chivas out of loyalty to his father.
- *Macaroni and Cheese*: Law partners in Jersey City, New Jersey, specializing in defending gamblers, purse snatchers, and Mafia hit men. They stay very busy.
- *Peanut Brittle*: Jockey from Paraguay. Last winner Peanut rode was Spanish Runner at Pimlico.
- *Ginger Snaps*: Apple Pan Dowdy's first cousin.

- *Eggs Benedict*: New York bookie.
- *Giblet Gravy*: Ringling Brothers midget. Lives in Sarasota, Florida, during winter season and works for Roto-Rooter.
- *Pepper Sauce*: Featured nude dancer at Atlanta's Gold Club.
- *Peach Preserves*: First runner-up behind Toffee Cake in the Miss Georgia pageant.
- *Stewed Tomatoes*: Real name of Otis Campbell, the loveable drunk on "The Andy Griffith Show."
- *Maple Butter*: Jimmy Swaggart's organist.
- *Liver and Onions*: Six o'clock evening news anchor team on WBRP–TV.
- *Noodle Soup*: Psychiatrist in the office of Noodle and Bean, P.C., in Augusta, Georgia.
- *Wild Rice*: A little South Carolina girl and Gary Hart's favorite dish.
- *Sinfully Rich Potato*: United States senator from Massachusetts.
- *Chicken Fricassee*: United States senator from Georgia.
- *Tutti Fruti Sherbet*: Former waiter at Cracker Barrel in Lebanon, Tennessee. Now lives in Atlanta with Fruit Medley.
- *Kidney Pie*: World renowned urologist in West Palm Beach, Florida.
- *Creamed Mushroom*: Atlanta Falcon linebacker.
- *Corn Flake Pastry*: Wrestler on TV's "World Championship Wrestling."
- *Fruit Punch*: Evander Holyfield's sparring partner. Lives in Atlanta with Fruit Medley and Tutti Frutti.
- *Cornbread Dressing*: Center for the New York Knicks, is 7'11" tall, and can jump over a water tank while holding a basketball in each hand.
- *Cherries Jubilee*: New Orleans streetwalker who plies her trade on Bourbon Street, also in Baton Rouge when Jimmy Swaggart is there.
- *Shrimp Scampi*: Cherries's business manager, who wears full-length leather coats, drives a Lincoln Continental, and an El Dorado, too. Has gold chains hanging from his Adam's apple to his navel, sterling silver dagger earrings in both ears, a Piaget watch, and is a close friend of Bad, Bad Leroy Brown.
- *Sour Dough*: Drug dealer from Colombia, now leasing Jim Bakker's Palm Springs, California, pad.
- *Brown 'n' Serve Rolls*: Lifeguard at Daytona Beach, Florida.

• *Roast Turkey*: Resident emcee at Ritz Carlton ballroom in Atlanta.

• *Chili Con Carne*: Operates a crap table in a Las Vegas gambling casino. Moonlights as a television evangelist in Los Angeles, hosting the "Lay You Two to One Rolling for Jesus" hour from 3:00 to 4:00 A.M. Sunday mornings before driving back to Vegas.

• *Yorkshire Pudding*: Breeder of champion thoroughbred terriers in Boston.

• *Chicken Cacciatore*: Racetrack tout in Maryland. Motto is "Have Handicap Sheet—Will Travel."

• *Tuna Rockefeller*: Niece of Nelson and first cousin of Oysters. Devoted tennis player. Is also a browser. Favorite browsing places are Tiffany, Saks Fifth Avenue, Nieman-Marcus, and Chase Manhattan Bank.

• *Quiche Lorraine*: Window dresser at Macy's. Had sex change operation in 1985 while spaced out on LSD.

• *Moo Goo Gai Pan*: Chinese English professor at Harvard. And at age seven, was the youngest Ph.D. on the Harvard faculty.

• *Cinnamon Buns*: Backup nude dancer to Hot Pepper Sauce at Atlanta's Gold Club.

A COMMUNICATIONS GAP
CAN MAKE A FELLA SICK

In the New Testament, Matthew 26:52, it is written: "Then said Jesus, all they that live by the sword shall die by the sword."

My friend Lewis Grizzard says, "Columnists live by the word and die by the word." Here's an example of what he does with words: "I am on call twenty-four hours a day. No story is ever too big or too small for a good columnist. If the bartender forgot to tell me the office called, however, it's not my fault."

I say that those of us who write newspaper columns and also profess to be public speakers live by the anecdote and die by the anecdote. Here's my example:

Years ago I heard a little anecdote that amused me. I memorized it. I've used it on many occasions since in speeches, especially at functions attended primarily by doctors and those associated with the medical field, such as nurses, druggists, medical technicians, and hospital office personnel.

Here's the anecdote . . .

A young doctor entering practice in a small south Georgia town after completing all his training rented office space in an old building in dire need of repair. After hiring a nurse and a receptionist, he was ready for the patients.

About midmorning of his first day of practice, a little old man dressed in work clothes walked in. He was greeted by the cheery receptionist.

"Hello! Can I help you, sir?"

"Uh, yessum. Just tell the doctor that I've got the shingles," he said meekly, hat in hand.

"Certainly. Just sign this register, note by your name what it is that you have, have a seat, and the doctor will be with you shortly," she instructed.

The little old man printed his name, wrote "shingles" next to it, and took a seat.

Shortly, the nurse appeared, called him by name, and asked that he follow her. Again, he did as he was told and followed her down a hallway until she stopped at the entrance to a small room.

"If you will just go in that room and remove your shirt, the doctor will be in shortly," she said. "Oh, by the way. Have you been to see any other doctor about your shingles?"

"No, ma'am. I was told to come here with 'em," he said meekly.

"Good! The doctor will be right with you. He's with a patient right now."

"Thank you, ma'am. I ain't in no hurry. This is the only stop I have scheduled today."

The little man removed his shirt, took a seat on the lone stool in the room, and waited . . . and waited . . . and waited.

Bye and bye the doctor came in. He also called the little man by name.

"Well, you say you've got the shingles, eh?"

"Yes, sir. I got 'em. A bunch of 'em."

"Let's have a look."

The little man had two small birthmarks on his left side just above the waistline. With a magnifying instrument, the doctor examined them and muttered a stifled "Hmmmmmmmm . . ." He then reached for his prescription pad and began scribbling. Finished, he handed the little man two prescriptions and said, "OK, you get these filled and take the medicine exactly as instructed. On your way out, after you pay the receptionist, ask her to make you an appointment. I'd like to see you again in three weeks."

"Yes, sir. But, uh . . ." the little man said.

"Just do as I told you!" snapped the young doctor and disappeared.

The little man put his shirt on, walked to the receptionist's desk, and relayed the doctor's instructions.

She tapped a pencil, eraser end down, on her desk as she reviewed the bare appointment book. "Hmmmmmmmm . . . how about, uh, let me see . . . Thursday, November 14th, at 11:00 A.M.? Will that be satisfactory?"

"I guess that's all right but . . ."

"Now then, do you prefer cash or check?"

"It don't really matter, but I got to ast you something . . ."

"Just pay first and then ask your question," she said.

The little man's meekness suddenly turned to stern determination. His jaw stiffened, his eyes narrowed, and he leaned toward the receptionist and said curtly, "Now you looka heah, ma'am. I've done ever' thing y'all ast me t' do. Now, I've got a question that th' doctor needs t' answer."

"What's your question?" the receptionist asked.

"All right. Would you be so kind as to go back there an' ast that doctor what he wants me to do with that load of shingles I got out back on my truck?"

There's a lesson to be learned by all this. Listen to the whole story because a communications gap really can make a fella sick.

GREAT TRAIN MISCOMMUNICATIONS

I had an uncle, Comer Jernigan, who was a conductor on the Central of Georgia Railroad for thirty-five years before his retirement. Long after retirement, railroading was still in his blood.

According to my grandfather, Wes Whaley, every time Uncle Comer heard a train whistle, he would instinctively reach for his official railroad watch, glance at it, and put it back in his watch pocket. But if somebody asked him the time, he would immediately reach for his watch again and check.

Uncle Comer would sit and tell railroad stories by the hour, and while these didn't originate with him, they have been around for many years. You may have heard them, but that's all right. So have I.

It seems that many years ago a man and his five-year-old son were passengers on a train. As the train roared through the countryside, the man would periodically turn and slap the youngster with the back of his hand.

Finally, after several such wallops, a well-dressed and obviously affluent woman sitting across the aisle reprimanded the man with this statement:

"Excuse me, but I must ask you to stop hitting that child. I am burdened with problems, plus I have a terrible headache. Somebody stole my mink coat, I ran my Rolls-Royce into a fire hydrant, my French poodle is ill, and four of my blue chip stocks dropped four points yesterday," she said. "With all these problems, surely you can understand why I am upset. And your repeated slapping of that youngster simply complicates my dilemma. I must ask that you stop."

The man hesitated, then turned and walloped the youngster again before addressing the woman.

"Problems? You say *you've* got problems? Lady, you don't know what problems are. Let me point out my problems to you," he said. "I'm on my way to the state prison to visit my oldest son who is being executed in the morning for murder. My wife ran off with the leader of a rock band last week and took my guitar and Ernest Tubb records with her. My youngest daughter is in a home for unwed mothers expecting a child in three weeks. On top of that, my IRS refund check bounced, I've got ingrown toenails, and my undershorts are too tight. I've got an abscessed wisdom tooth, and my brother-in-law is suing me for wrecking his pickup truck. Plus, this young 'un has messed up his pants, eaten the tickets, and on top of all that I'm on the wrong train! And you say *you* have problems?"

An exchange of letters between a nervous man who lived next to a railroad yard and the local railroad agent:

Gentlemen,
    Why is it that your engine has to ding and dong and fizz and spit and bang and hiss and pant and grate and grind and puff and hump and chug and hoot and whistle and snarl and growl and boom and crash and jolt and screech and throb and roar and rattle and grunt and strain and tug and tear and stop and start all night long when I'm trying to sleep?

After due deliberation the local railroad agent penned these words in the form of a reply to the complaining resident:

Dear Sir,
    In reply to your recent letter regarding noise made by our trains:
    Sorry, but if you are to get vital needs including meats and sweets and breads and spreads and guns and buns and beans and jeans and shirts and skirts and shirts and blouses and socks and locks and booze and shoes and dippers and slippers and lotions and notions and candy bars and nuts in jars and sugar and spice and everything nice to make you happy all your life and satisfy the fancy of your devoted wife . . . you really shouldn't criticize the noise made by our trains.

Making fun of the slowness of trains has long been an American tradition. Like the story of the woman and her husband who boarded the train in Atlanta en route to Washington, D.C.

En route, the woman gave birth to a baby just outside Richmond, Virginia. When the ordeal was over, the obviously annoyed conducter castigated the new mother, saying: "Young lady, you never should have boarded this train knowing you were in that condition."

The young mother retorted, "Well, when my husband and I boarded this train, I wasn't in that condition."

The old gentleman had never before ridden a train. He approached the ticket window at the Jacksonville, Florida, station and said, "I'd like a round-trip ticket, please."

"Where to?" grunted the ticket agent.

"Back here."

The little old lady had never before ridden a train. She boarded and took a seat by the window.

Shortly, the conductor came by taking up tickets. The little old lady searched diligently in her handbag for hers. In the process, she dropped an apple and a banana, broke a bottle of Milk of Magnesia that saturated the conductor's trousers, watched a ball of yarn roll from one end of the railroad car to the other, dropped $2.45 in change under the seat, stabbed the conductor in the groin with a knitting needle while trying to recover the money, and spilled a bottle of aspirin in the aisle. Still, no ticket.

Feeling that she should offer some explanation, she said to the conductor, "You know, I've never ridden the train before."

"Yes, ma'am," the conductor agreed. "We ain't missed you, either."

TREASURES OF BOTCHED
COMMUNICATION

I keep on my desk a little box. I call it my trivia box. It contains written reminders of stories either sent or related to me. Here are a few of my favorite treasures.

A Matter of Survival

A woman from South Georgia went to Atlanta to see the governor about getting her husband out of prison.

"What's he in for?" asked the governor.

"For stealin' a ham."

"That doesn't seem too bad. Is he a good worker?"

"No, suh. To tell ya th' truth, he's purty lazy."

"Oh. Well, he's good to you and the children, isn't he?"

"Not really. He's purty mean to us."

"How many children do you have?"

"Eight, with 'nother 'un due in two months."

"Is he a steady worker?"

"Nope. He don't work."

"Then why would you want a man like that out of prison and back home?"

"Well, Governor, it's like this. We've done run outta ham."

Some People Talk Funny

Highlands, North Carolina, is the summer home of thousands of Yankees who migrate there each June from New Jersey and New York by way of West Palm Beach, Florida, and stay until mid-October, then return to West Palm Beach.

One afternoon late in October, a man from Massachusetts stopped at a service station in Highlands on his way to Florida for the winter. It was his first time ever in the South.

"Tell me, young man," he said to the station attendant, "Where can I find some of those people around here who talk so funny?"

"You're too late, mister," the attendant replied. "They ain't none heah now."

"None here? Why not?"

"They done all went back to Florida f'r th' winter."

Everybody's Gotta' Be Somewhere

She left him on the sofa when the telephone rang and was back in a few seconds.

"Who was it?" he asked nervously.

"My husband," she replied calmly.

"Your husband! Where was he calling from?" he shouted in a near-panic tone.

"Relax," she said, patting him on the hand. "He won't be home for another three or four hours."

"How can you be so sure?"

"Because he's at the club . . . playing poker with you."

A Party Argument

A Republican husband and his Democrat wife rode in silence for hours following a heated political argument. Neither would budge. Finally, the husband pointed to a jackass in a pasture.

"Relative of yours?" he asked sarcastically.

"Yes," she replied. "By marriage."

Prelude to Manslaughter

The scrawny little fellow walked into a bar, ordered a margarita, and asked the burly bartender if he enjoyed dumb-jock jokes.

"Listen, shrimp," the bartender growled. "See them two big guys at the end of the bar? Them's both defensive linemen for the Atlanta Falcons. See the fella at th' pinball machine? He's a professional 'rassler. An' th' one by the jukebox readin' a comic book is a world champion weightlifter. An' 'nother thing. I played tackle f'r th' Pittsburgh Steelers f'r nine years. Now then, you still wanna' tell your dumb-jock joke here?"

"Nah, I guess not."

"No guts, eh?"

"Oh, it's not that."

"No? What then?"

"I just wouldn't want to have to explain it five times."

Yuppies Are Indeed Different

A yuppie was driving his new BMW convertible around Atlanta with his left arm hanging over the side and his tape player going full blast. A garbage truck pulled around him, sideswiped his BMW, and kept going.

The yuppie pulled to a stop, observed the damage to the side of his BMW, and in a frantic rage cried out, "My car! My beautiful car!"

Shortly, a policeman came by and the yuppie told him about the accident.

"Look! My beautiful BMW is a wreck!" he shouted.

"You've got more than your car to worry about, buddy," the policeman said. "You need an ambulance. Look at your left arm."

The yuppie looked at his badly injured and bleeding left arm and cried out, "My Rolex! My beautiful Rolex!"

SECTION FIVE

LIFE IS GETTIN'
CONFUSING

HAVE YOU READ YOUR AUTOMOBILE OWNER'S MANUAL?

I must trade cars with more frequency than Zsa Zsa and Elizabeth Taylor trade husbands. Like the husbands, I usually get taken. A good car trader I'm not.

I've owned automobiles since 1947, including a 1965 Mercury Marauder named Maude that was almost like a member of the family for years and years before giving out and being admitted to the Intensive Car Unit. I still miss Maude. She was a good old girl, and loyal to the end. My heart aches even now when I pass ICU and see her just sitting out in the cold.

As of this writing, I'm driving a 1988 Buick Riviera that I bought from two good friends, Jan and Randy Mimbs. That was a mistake. Never buy a car from good friends. It was presented to me as Jan's car with "very low mileage." I learned why shortly after buying it: She only drove it when she could get it started.

It is the only car I've ever owned that has a mind of its own. Everything is controlled by a computer, which Jan took the time to explain, along with the sixteen-way seat, collapsible steering wheel, and even reversible upholstery affording the choice of leather or velour. But she kept skirting the issue every time I inquired about the motor, except to say, "Oh, it has one! It's a very nice car, and I'm enjoying it."

The car has one feature, however, that Jan neglected to mention or explain. I call it a burglar alarm, but that ain't really technically correct. The owner's manual identifies it as the Theft Deterrent System. Therein lies the reason that I say the car has a mind of its own. The Theft Deterrent System activates when and where it gets darn good and ready to activate.

I had never owned an automobile with a Theft Deterrent System. I had never owned an automobile with reversible leather/velour upholstery, either. And I had never read an automobile owner's manual from cover to cover until recently. I know now that I should have read it immediately after buying the car. This fact came through *loud* and clear on a trip to Tennessee and Kentucky shortly after I purchased it.

Here are three reasons why I should have read the manual and/or Jan should have told me about the Theft Deterrent System:

I pulled into a crowded parking garage in Knoxville, Tennessee, near the University of Tennessee at the height of rush hour traffic. Cars were jammed in. So were people, all trying to leave at the same time. I was trying to leave with them. I stopped at the pay booth, pulled a parking ticket taken from a ticket dispensing machine two hours earlier, lowered my window, reached my arm toward the toll collector, brushed the side view mirror with my hand and dropped the ticket. This, of course, necessitated my opening the door to reach down and retrieve it. That is when *it* happened.

My horn commenced to blow at the rate of fifty times per minute. The headlights and parking lights followed suit, blinking at the same rate as the horn was blowing, reminiscent of the famous jailbreak scene in the 1939 movie *The Big House* starring George Raft and James Cagney.

A little old lady, bless her heart, standing in front of my Buick Riviera jumped over the hood of a Jaguar XJ6. Her husband followed suit, his briefcase landing on the top of the toll booth and he on the trunk of a Mercedes 300SL.

My Buick Riviera continued to do its thing for seven *long* minutes while I sat inside. I know it was seven minutes because I later read it in the operator's manual that I should have read two weeks earlier when I bought the car.

The scene repeated two days later, at about 2:30 A.M., in the parking lot at a Holiday Inn near Lexington, Kentucky. Lord, it can be quiet and still in a motel parking lot near Lexington, Kentucky, at 2:30 in the morning.

Motel room lights came on. Eyes peeked out from behind drapes and through slightly opened doors. Surely, they must have concluded, a raid was in progress. Explanations by the dozens surely were being dreamed up.

For seven long minutes I'm sure there were seriously concerned guests. When my Theft Deterrent System finally stopped, the other guests must have been relieved as they watched me walk to my room.

The next catastrophe came in the parking lot at Hamilton Place Mall in Chattanooga, Tennessee. That time I took the easy way out, walking away from my little Buick and pretending not to know the dummy who owned the honking and blinking Riviera. I ducked into the nearest coffee shop and waited seven minutes before casually and nonchalantly strolling back to my car.

The crowd had dispersed, with the exception of a woman and her two screaming and scared-slap-to-death children who thought Armageddon had begun. I had escaped detection, and probably mob violence.

I've had my Buick Riviera, the "Dennis the Menace" of automobiles, for a little over a year now. I'm convinced that its Theft Deterrent System is programmed to activate in at least three places:

- Behind any funeral procession.
- Behind any semitrailer truck driven by a man six feet, eight inches tall and weighing in at 296 who can't stand it when people behind him blow their horn when he is stopped at a red light.
- In the immediate vicinity of any Ku Klux Klan demonstration or Gay Rights Liberation Movement protest, thereby signaling to the world my support for the same.

I've learned how to deactivate the Buick Riviera's Theft Deterrent Device like the manual instructs. Just insert the door key in the lock on the driver's side and turn it one-quarter turn clockwise. My problem is, it takes me more than seven minutes to locate the key among all the junk in my pocket.

A word of advice from one who's been there: Take the time to read your automobile owner's manual. You will be amazed at what you will learn about your car.

I'LL NEVER UNDERSTAND DIVESTITURE

Every month I receive a crossword puzzle in my mailbox. It is the brainchild of Southern Bell Telephone Company and AT&T. I've never understood crossword puzzles, and I don't understand the puzzle that comes monthly from Southern Bell and AT&T. Like everybody else, I just send a check along in order to keep my telephone ringing.

The whole puzzle started with government-approved divestiture, and we know from long years of experience that anything even remotely associated with government is going to be messed up. That's what divestiture did. It screwed up the nation's telephone systems. Alexander Graham Bell is probably still turning over and over in his grave. Even he, as brilliant as he was, could never decipher today's telephone bill.

My telephone bill used to consist of two pages. It was simple. Basic charges were listed on one page, and long distance charges were on the other. Those days are gone forever. My telephone bill now runs six or seven pages, and that's before I get to the long distance calls!

I just happen to have one I haven't paid yet, but will. Decipher it? No. Pay it? Yes. As I look it over I know it's absolutely folly for me to try and understand it. I can, however, figure out where my money goes. Everybody gets a slice of the telephone pie. Beginning on page one, here's what my bill looks like:

• Page one of thirteen, line one: "Total amount due $72.20." Line two: "Current charges. See page two." So, on to page two:

• Page two: Here's what it looks like.
"Detail of current charges."
"Southern Bell Monthly Service . . . $12.05"
"Itemized calls . . . See page 5. $37.00"

"Tax: Federal . . . $1.46"
"State—Local: 47 cents . . . $1.93"
"Southern Bell Current Charges . . . $50.98"
All finished with page two. Let's move along to page three:

• Page three: Again, Detail of Current Charges, AT&T Information Systems.
   "Monthly equipment . . . $2.85."
   "Tax: Federal . . . 9 cents; State and Local . . . 12 cents."

• Page four told me this:
"Detail of current charges, AT&T Communications"
"Itemized calls—See page eleven . . . $17.63."
"Tax: Federal . . . 53 cents."
"AT&T Communications Current Charges . . . $18.16."

• Pages five through ten were a repeat of the previous information. Why, I'll never know. Probably to verify that after having gone through the first four pages, I had developed double vision. Look at this, appearing on the bottom of page ten:
   "Southern Bell Total Charge for Itemized Calls . . . $37.00"
   "Total Tax: Federal . . . $1.11. State .00. (That was confusing. What happened to the 47 cents state tax listed on pages two and three?)

• Pages eleven and twelve contained this vital information:
"AT&T Communications Long Distance Calls, Itemized."
   "AT&T Communications Total Charge For Long Distance Calls . . . $17.63."
   "Total Tax: Federal . . . 53 cents. State . . . 00." (And, there we go again.)

• Page thirteen concluded the book with this bit of vital information that I just couldn't do without:
   "Key: Rate Applied."
   "DC: DAY CLG CD."
   "EC: Evening CLG CD."
   "DS: Day Station."
   "NC: Night, WKND CLG CD."

By this time I had triple vision and a headache.

The way I figure it, it's like this: Out of my $72.20 pie, Southern Bell got a slice; AT&T Information Systems got a slice; AT&T Communications got a slice; Uncle Sam got a slice, small though it was; the state of Georgia got a slice, but barely enough to taste; and I didn't get a crumb.

Who got what? I ain't that smart. All I know is that should you dial my number and get a recording that says, "We're sorry, this number has been temporarily disconnected while Southern Bell, AT&T Information Systems, AT&T Communications, Uncle Sam, and the state of Georgia fight over who gets what percentage of the customer's $72.20 check. It is anticipated that this dispute will be settled in the near future. If you have been inconvenienced, we apologize. However, our error-proof computer should have this customer's service restored soon. Thank you . . . This is a recording . . . This is a recording . . . This is a recording . . . This is a . . ." You can rest assured that if the problem isn't resolved soon, I can always go to arbitration. I might just do that.

A LOOK AT THE TIES THAT BLIND

Let's face it, men's ties they're selling today are awful. Television personalities top the list of people who wear the ugliest ties. And have you ever noticed that the wealthiest men wear outlandish ties? They do indeed wear the ties that blind.

I'm pretty conservative when it comes to ties. Just a small stripe, a paisley design with muted twirls, or a small, barely visible blending check will do. I don't care for a tie with Niagara Falls, the Washington Monument, or Mount Vesuvius erupting all over it.

The last time I tried to select and buy a tie, my mind erupted. The ones I had hanging on my tie rack at home were as conservative as a nun's habit compared to the ones hanging on the racks in the fashionable Atlanta men's store where I was shopping.

I made my way through the shirts, pants, sport coats, suits, and underwear before turning a corner and coming face to face with a bank of what had to be the ugliest ties I'd ever seen.

I questioned the clerk, who was wearing a kaleidoscope, regarding the unusual and, to me, repulsive designs on the ties.

"They're in vogue this year," he told me, with a somewhat haughty air.

"Not with me," I countered. "To me they're not in vogue, they're in trouble."

He walked away and began, unnecessarily, rearranging the neat stacks of underwear.

It was like visiting an abstract art exhibit as I stood before the bank of ties and studied them at length. I concluded that the works of Picasso and Dali would have been too conservative to make the tie rack.

I also reached a certain conclusion regarding ties in general and today's ties in particular.

- Ties ain't really necessary. Like the IRS, they choke you to death and serve no useful purpose.
- Ties only serve to get caught in zippers and dragged through gravy.
- Ties today are priced in about the same range as a Mercedes.
- Ties are designed by men who were either mentally ill or highly intoxicated—or both—at the time they designed them.
- Ties never stay straight.
- Ties only serve two useful purposes: for making quilts and as a tourniquet in case of a medical emergency.

I looked over the ties in the Atlanta store. This is what I saw:

- I saw a tie that looked like it had been dipped in a bucket of Louisiana pinks.
- I saw a tie that strongly resembled a salad bar.
- I saw a tie that looked like some guy had dropped his breakfast all over it.
- I saw a tie with eyes all over it. It was a not-so-delicate mix of chartreuse, lavender, and pink lines, all intertwined. And I'm pretty sure one of the eyes winked at me.
- I saw a tie that even a rock singer wouldn't wear, and that's a clock-stopping ugly tie.
- I saw a tie that looked like a Las Vegas crap table. It was a loser, featuring nothing but snake eyes on the dice.
- I saw a tie that looked like a plane crash.
- I saw a tie that looked like a bowl of shrimp.
- I saw a tie that looked like the aftermath of a hurricane.
- I saw a tie that looked like a hazardous-waste dump site.
- I saw a tie that looked like a closet full of wire coat hangers, naturally all intermingled and twisted.
- I saw a tie that looked like it had chicken pox. The one hanging next to it had measles, I think. But then, chicken pox is contagious.

• I saw a tie that looked like it had quotation marks all over it. I waited but it never said anything.

Needless to say, I didn't buy a tie in that shop. I decided to just hold on to the ones I have. They'll probably be back in vogue within a year or two. If not, I'll just dip some in a bucket of Louisiana pinks and drag the others through a salad bar.

WHAT YOU SEE AIN'T ALWAYS WHAT YOU GET

I spend very little time in supermarkets. Well, that's not exactly true. I spend a heck of a lot of time in supermarkets, most of it in line at the checkout attempting to post bond and get out or waiting for the cashier to break into a new roll of pennies. I'll never understand why, but when it's my turn to pay, the cashier is always out of pennies.

I've reached the point where I play games in supermarkets. A favorite is to walk the aisles looking at the cans and cartons that house the goodies, especially those with pictures on the outside of what's supposed to be on the inside. But whatever happened to truth in advertising?

I know a man in Florida who wrote the CEO of a giant corporation to complain that the peas inside the can didn't even remotely resemble the peas pictured on the label of the can he bought.

The CEO responded, saying he was sorry the man was disappointed and enclosed certificates for four complimentary cans of the same brand of peas.

"They didn't look any better," the man said.

Walk the aisles and take a look. What you see ain't always what you get.

Here are a few of my observations:

• *Frozen biscuits*: The biscuits pictured on the can look like they just came out the winner in a Best Biscuit Baking Contest. So light and fluffy. But open the can, and you'll find them all twisted, stuck together, and hard to separate. When you do separate them, place them on a baking sheet, and shove 'em in the oven to bake, you get what, for lack of a better word, are diversified biscuits. Some will be the size of quarters while others compare favorably to manhole covers.

- *Frozen pound cake*: Look at the picture closely. Surely the cake was made in heaven. No doubt the company commissioned Rembrandt to paint its picture on the outside of the box. It will really bring your tastebuds to life. OK. So you buy it, take it home, heat it, and take it out of the oven. You end up with a humpback pound cake that's split down the middle and refuses to come off the aluminum-wrapped piece of cardboard on which it rests.

- *Frozen pies*: I challenge you to show me a more beautiful pie—be it apple, lemon, coconut, chocolate, or whatever—than is depicted on frozen pie boxes. Since Rembrandt is already under contract to the frozen pound cake makers, the frozen pie folks must have commissioned Renoir to paint their masterpieces. Open the box, and what do you see? Looks like something Picasso or Dali would have done, with everything running together, drippy and sticky.

- *Pizza*: I don't even eat pizza, but the pictures on the boxes would make me fight for one. They all look like Tony just removed them from the oven. But open one up and take a look at all the little dead, frozen, and whiskered anchovies lying around. They look like the victims of an oil spill.

    Caution: Never look at a frozen pizza with anchovies until it comes out of the microwave oven. Some wise man once said there are two things people don't need to see being made: laws and sausage. Add pizza as a third consideration.

- *Grits*: The picture of the steaming hot bowl of grits on the box looks so inviting you want to run right home and begin heating the water, but it doesn't show the lumps. My grits always have lumps.

- *Broccoli*: Sorry, even the best photograph or the most talented artist can't help broccoli. While it is the exception, what you see is what you get with broccoli.

    And have you ever taken a close look at an Irish potato? Irish potatoes probably outsell every other item in the supermarket. It has always been a mystery to me how anything so ugly can be made to taste so good in so many different ways.

BEING A CONVERSATION CAPTIVE IS NO FUN

While I don't understand it, there are those who are convinced that engaging another in conversation when both are in captive surroundings is a required activity. What are captive surroundings? They are places where you happen to be and can't escape, such as elevators, airplanes, lunch counters, waiting rooms, stadium bleachers, rest rooms, and bank teller lines.

Being caught in captive surroundings happens to me with alarming regularity. I can think of several instances right off the bat:

• *Coffee Shops*: Recently I was seated on a stool at a lunch counter in a coffee shop in a strange town. A man came in, chose the stool next to me, sat down, and ordered coffee. Before he had put cream and sugar in it, he proceeded to tell me in no uncertain terms what was wrong with the Social Security system in America.

I was a captive, with the choice of abandoning my fresh cup of coffee, leaving and finding another coffee shop, or staying to listen to a lengthy discourse as an unwilling student in his Social Security 101 class. I chose the latter but flunked the course when I finally disagreed with his theories on the subject.

• *Elevators*: You are in the basement of a sixteen-story office building and push the button for the fifteenth floor. One other person steps on and pushes the button for the twelfth floor. Know how he starts the conversation? And bear in mind that you are in the basement.

"Goin' up?" he asks.

If he were going to the fifteenth floor, too, do you know what he'd do right after you push 15? Right, he'd follow suit and push it, too. Why? Would that make the elevator go twice as fast?

• *Airplanes*: I doubt that there is any more captive surrounding than being a passenger on a commercial airline. Let's assume I'm flying from Atlanta to New York. This is how it usually goes with me:

I select seat number C–27, which is the center seat in a cluster of three. I really want W–27 (window) or A–27 (aisle), but inasmuch as these are spoken for by the time I arrive at the loading gate because I lost over an hour trying to find the Atlanta airport exit off I-285, I settle for C–27, a loser.

So, there I sit in C–27, seat belt fastened as required and newspaper in my lap as desired, when W–27 and A–27 arrive. W–27 is a recently paroled former rock band cocaine junkie turned born-again Christian on his way to New York to team up with a TV evangelist for a crusade. He will serve his apprenticeship en route to having his own TV ministry and spread the message from pillar to post: send money. He chooses to practice his spiel on me, but the cross—approximating the size of the *Queen Mary*'s anchor—hanging on a chain around his neck keeps getting in the way.

A–27 is heading home to mama in Brooklyn after throwing in the towel on a twelve-year marriage that produced seven kids, "because he gave me very little attention and made me feel neglected." (What? Seven kids . . . twelve-year marriage . . . very little attention . . . neglected. Hmmmmmm.)

Our flight isn't three minutes off the runway before I become—unwillingly—her marriage counselor. I listen to her and nod all the way to Richmond, Virginia, before W–27 relieves me. From Richmond to New York neither W–27 or A–27 speaks to me. They speak *across* me. Being a victim caught in captive surroundings, I'm forced to listen to all the gory details of an unhappy marriage and the pitfalls of cocaine addiction.

I think A–27 and W–27 were engaged when the airplane touched down at LaGuardia Airport. I wished them both well and breathed a sigh of relief.

• *Waiting rooms*: How do you handle it when you're seated in a filled-to-capacity waiting room at your dentist's office with a right jaw that looks like you're chewing on a grapefruit, and the guy seated next to you wants to talk? All you really want is to die or get relief. He comes on with, "Whatsa matter? You got a toothache?" and you're in so much pain it hurts to grunt.

And what about the character that comes in and sits next to you while you're waiting to see your doctor? Your right arm is in a cast up to your right armpit. What does he ask? You got it: "Didja hurt y'r arm?"

• *Football stadiums*: Here's one you can count on. There you sit in the south stands, Section 135, Aisle 66, Row Z, Seat 50, so far removed from what's going on down on the football field that the game is nothing more than a rumor. And here *he* comes, the holder of the ticket to Seat 49.

He's decked out in black trousers with a miniature Bulldog emblazoned on the left front pocket, a red shirt with the dog's twin brother sitting over the pocket, a red-and-black cap flashing "Go Dawgs" on the front, and carrying a red and black umbrella, a portable radio, and a container of liquid. The guy is so much a Bulldog he doesn't, when introduced to you, shake hands. He runs around back and sniffs the seat of your pants.

Even before taking his seat, he declares his loyalty, saying, "I'm for them Dawgs, buddy. How 'bout choo?" He then makes three circles, takes his seat, and proceeds to explain in detail the game plan, including why the coach should have run for the U.S. Senate and the pedigree of every Bulldog on the field. The entire litter, all ninety-five of 'em!

From the initial kickoff to the final gun at game's end, he's one step ahead of the Bulldog cheerleaders. He may be the only person among the 85,000 in attendance who knows all the words to the alma mater.

When the game is over, he'll follow you all the way out of the stadium and across the parking lot telling you how and why the Bulldogs won, or lost.

• *Restrooms*: This situation always presents a problem for me. I never know just what to say when standing shoulder to waistline with "The Incredible Hulk." Like when he glances over and asks, "You fum Chicago, buddy?"

"No, sir." I answered weakly. "But I'll move there if you want me to."

I've always enjoyed the story about the stranger who attempted to initiate a conversation with a junkie standing on a Los Angeles street corner.

The stranger stopped, pointed to the sky, and said, "Say,

fella, is that the sun or the moon up there?"

Without bothering to raise his head, the junkie replied: "I don't know, man. I don't live around here."

SOME EMPLOYEES WILL NEVER GET THE PICTURE

I'll be the first to admit that I'm not the most patient and understanding man in the world. I could name people from all over who would attest to it and furnish sworn statements.

I am most impatient, and the least understanding, when waiting for a service that I intend to pay for or have already paid for. Also with business establishments that employ incompetent people. Here are two examples:

The first happened in Savannah, Georgia, but it could have happened anywhere. It just so happened that Savannah is where I happened to be when the seat of my britches split as I got back in my car after pumping ten dollars' worth of unleaded gasoline into the gas tank, fourteen cents' worth on my shoes, and another dime's worth on my right pants leg.

I was on my way to a meeting and immediately began searching for a place to get my britches sewn up. I have a thing about speaking to ladies while decked out in split britches.

I spotted a place within fifteen minutes, "Martha's Stitch and Sew Shop."

After wheeling into the parking lot, I rushed inside to see Martha, sensing a strong wind blowing from the south as I trotted to the front door, opened it, and heard a little bell ring that alerted all on the premises to the fact that I had arrived sporting split britches that smelled strongly of unleaded gasoline.

However, the bell didn't faze the only employee in the shop. She was on the telephone and continued her conversation without so much as a nod to verify that she knew I was there. I stood at the counter, alternately on my unleaded right leg and my dry left one.

I heard but one side of the telephone conversation: "Naw,

we ain't goin'. Jeff's done seen it twice't. An' I learned that Lori's baby is due nex' week so that means I'll be workin' a double shift startin' Monday. An', 'nother thing . . ."

Finally, it was my turn. "Hol' on a minute, Carol. They's some guy heah. Lemme see what he wants."

She propped the receiver on her left shoulder, anchored it with her chin, lit another Virginia Slim, and said, "Ya want somethin', mister?"

My initial reaction was to tell her that I only came in to watch my fingernails grow, but thought better of that when I noticed by the clock on the wall that the time was 5:55 P.M. and I still had thirty-five miles to drive for a 7:00 P.M. meeting.

"Yes, I split my britches in the seat and . . ." I started.

"Martha ain't heah," she interrupted. "Y'll have to come back t'morrow."

"But I need . . ."

"I don' do no sewin'," she said. "Y'll jus' have t' come back t'morrow."

"No, you're wrong!" I told her with fixed jaw. "I don't *have* to come back here at all! And I'm not!"

With that I left, drove three miles down the road to Luther's Bargain Store, and invested $24.95, plus tax, in a pair of off-brand blue trousers. I then drove to the meeting, spoke to the ladies, and on my way back thumbed my nose at Martha's Stitch and Sew as I passed. I glanced at my watch. It was 9:50 P.M. The old gal was still inside, talking on the telephone.

Who knows? Maybe Lori's baby came early, and so did the old gal's double shift.

My next happening came in South Carolina at a fast-food establishment, and only as a last resort do I patronize fast-food restaurants. This was a case of last resort. I was hungry.

It was while waiting in line to order that I concluded that many fast-food waitresses can't operate the dadgummed cash register. It's not really their fault, however. The way fast-food establishment cash registers are designed, it almost takes somebody with a Ph.D. in computer science to get one of the things open. I don't know any fast-food waitresses with a Ph.D. in computer science.

First, the waitress must punch eleven buttons, insert a secret code known but to herself, the manager, and God, cancel out all previous errors, start over, say a little prayer, call for help, and then watch all the other employees gather around for the grand cash register opening, if there is to be one.

I waited, waited, and waited until the tape was changed, the cash drawer replaced, and a shift change made. I still hadn't ordered. It really didn't matter because I ain't too keen on eating in no place that has a sign as big as a sheet of plywood on the wall behind the counter announcing for the entire world to see:

"Condiments Available Upon Request."

I'm just too old-fashioned and set in my ways for that. I'm from the old school and firmly believe such things should be kept underneath the counter, out of sight, and dispensed only to consenting adults.

I know my patience is short, but I'm convinced that society has just become too permissive.

THE PARTY'S GREAT,
BUT THE GUEST LIST AIN'T EASY

Everybody loves a party. I know people in the South who will throw a party at the drop of a sausage ball.

I'd never really considered all the preparation that goes into party planning until I overheard a discussion between two ladies planning one while having lunch.

The refreshments are no problem. The guest list, I learned, is another bowl of dip.

I was sitting alone. Two tables away the ladies were working on the guest list. I didn't intentionally eavesdrop, but I couldn't help but hear this conversation:

"What about Marlo?"

"Goodness, no! We can't have Marlo and Matt at the same party. They've only been divorced four months, the property is still in litigation, and Matt—jerk that he is—is balking on the amount of alimony and child support."

"Oh, I didn't know about that. Scratch Marlo. How about Howard?"

"Well, if we invite Howard, we'll have to scratch Bert."

"Why?"

"Because Howard coaches the Little League team that Bert's son Jimmy plays on. Bert challenged Howard to a fight three weeks ago after Howard waved Jimmy around third base and he was thrown out twelve feet from home plate. Bert called Howard a dumbass for sending Jimmy home, and Howard told Bert that Jimmy was an idiot for not sliding. Then Geneva, Bert's wife, threw a slice of pizza, with anchovies, at Howard and hit him in the neck. That's when Rhonda, Howard's wife, snatched the cushion from Geneva that she'd loaned her to sit on and screamed that she couldn't sit on it anymore."

"So much for Howard and Bert. Scratch both of 'em. What about Kathy?"

"Not if we invite Jan."

"Oh? Why not?"

"Do you remember that yellow dress with the purple tulips and candy canes that Kathy wore to Carla's graduation last month?"

"Do I remember it? Ugliest dress ever! And she wears it to everything."

"Right. Well, Theresa . . . you know Theresa who works at the Better Bargain Discount Store . . . told me at the super-market that Jan bought one exactly like it and can't wait to wear it. So what if she should wear it to our party and sees Kathy in hers? And you just know Kathy is going to wear hers, right?"

"No doubt about that. Scratch Kathy. Who else?"

"You know we are obligated to invite Helen. She invited us to her bon voyage party when she and Lewis went on that cheap three-day cruise to Nassau and Helen brought back all that cheap perfume with the counterfeit labels and then tried to pay for the cruise by selling it. Remember?"

"Heck yeah, I remember! I paid her eighteen dollars for a bottle of Giorgio that turned out to be Passionate Possum that she paid only $1.75 for. But we can't invite Helen if Louise is coming, you know."

"Louise? Why?"

"Because they're not speaking, that's why."

"Oh."

"You know how Helen brags on her oyster casserole, right?"

"Honey, the whole world knows that."

"Well, Helen won first place in the Best Cook Contest with it last March. Louise came in fourth with her sweet potato soufflé. It wouldn't do to have Helen and Louise in the same room, or the same building for that matter."

"I heard that!"

"Now then, do you have Archie on your list?"

"I did, but I scratched his name off."

"You did?"

"Yeah. I had to."

"Reason?"

"Because of that Jaguar XJ12 he bought in Florida."

"Something wrong with the Jag?"

"Oh, no! It's gorgeous. But at the hospital, the golf course, the bowling alley—everywhere—he always parks it right next to Leon's ten-year-old beat-up BMW just to aggravate him. And I've heard that Leon says if Archie doesn't stop it, one of these days he's going to kick the door in and break all the windows."

"Not at our party, he won't! Delete either Archie or Leon, or both."

When I left the restaurant, the ladies were still deleting and scratching. My name wasn't mentioned, so I probably won't get an invitation and will never know who *was* invited.

MY OWN RATING SYSTEMS

In the past I have served as a judge at beauty contests, barbecue cookoffs, homecoming parades, disco dance competitions, cake-baking contests, Halloween costume contests, cutest girl photo contest for *Seventeen* magazine, and most beautiful baby contests. (A word of caution here: *Never* agree to serve as the only judge in a baby contest because in the eyes of the parents and grandparents, there just ain't no such things as an ugly baby.)

Rating systems vary with the event. Some prefer the "Poor, Good, Very Good, Excellent" rating system. Others employ the "First, Second, Third, Fourth" system. But probably the most popular, and the one I prefer, is the "1 to 10" system, 10 representing the best and 1 the lowest.

Ratings are big, and not only in contests. Politicians are constantly concerned with ratings that go up and down like an elevator. And approval or disapproval ratings resulting from polls can and do alter the decisions of elected officials.

I first began considering ratings after thumbing through a trade magazine at a radio station and learned that radio stations are rated by Arbitron. In television it's the Nielsen ratings that are all-important.

Both Arbitron and Nielsen ratings determine what rate advertisers will pay for radio and television advertising. It's simple: The more listeners or viewers, the higher the advertising rate. With newspapers, it's different. Circulation is the gauge with newspapers.

Movies are rated G, PG, R, X, and sometimes XXX, depending on the content of the movie.

Dunn and Bradstreet deals in credit ratings, a AAA rating being tops.

Consumer's Guide rates merchandise.

Hotels are rated by stars, the best designated *****. Likewise with restaurants.

Even one movie star, Bo Derek, was once rated a 10. That's understandable. The movie was titled after her 10 rating.

I have a good friend who rates people by assigning a batting average. If a person is unusual, exceptionally talented, handsome or beautiful, or a strange character, my friend assigns a .400 rating. I've heard him say on many occasions of someone being discussed or passing by, "Now then, there's a .400 hitter."

I'm convinced that all of us, albeit subconsciously at times, tend to assign ratings to people and things. I know I do, using the "1 to 10" rating system. Here are a few of them:

- Jukeboxes in fast-food establishments (1)
- Jane Fonda (2)
- Henry Fonda (9)
- Homemade biscuits (10)
- Frozen biscuits (4)
- Susan B. Anthony dollars (1)
- Nashville, Tennessee (10)
- Rush Limbaugh (2)
- Paul Harvey (10)
- Vanilla ice cream (9)
- Liver (1)
- October (10)
- February (3)
- Birmingham, Alabama (9)
- I–40 between Knoxville, Tennessee, and Asheville, North Carolina (10)
- The Jacksonville, Florida, *Times Union* (10)
- Dave Barry (1)
- Jimmy Carter, the man (8)
- President Jimmy Carter (1)
- Rock music (-1)
- Madonna (-1)
- Atlanta, Georgia (2)
- Earrings on men (1)
- Grits (10)
- Cream of wheat (2)
- Dedicated waitresses (9)
- Accomplished cooks (9)

- April 15 (1)
- Ice water (9)
- Classroom teachers (10)
- Friends (7)
- Good friends (10)
- Computers, when they're up (10)
- Computers, when they're down (1)
- Dedicated preachers (10)
- Religious radio and television quacks soliciting money in the name of the Lord (-1)
- Hot-air hand dryers in public rest rooms (1)
- Cokes in cans (5)
- Cokes in six-ounce bottles (10)
- Destin, Florida (10)
- Paid bills (10)
- Unpaid bills (5)
- Overdue bills (1)
- Chitlins (1)
- Vienna sausages (9)
- Country ham (10)
- Barbecued ribs (10)
- Pay day (10)
- A queen when you need a king (1)
- Scotch tape (8)
- Kleenex (8)
- Roseanne Barr (-1)
- Clean sheets (9)
- Pornography (-2)
- Fridays (9)
- Saturdays (8)
- Sundays (10)
- Mondays (1)
- Plastic tabs that fasten price tags to clothing (-1)
- Graduation (10)
- Small towns (8)
- Telephone solicitors (1)
- Grandchildren (10)

SECTION SIX

BUT I DO UNDERSTAND SOME THINGS

THINGS I DO UNDERSTAND

I'm very fortunate. Thank God, I know that. I live the good life. I enjoy good health, have great friends, two fine children, two fine grandchildren, an outstanding son-in-law and daughter-in-law, a comfortable house, a little backyard, and a swing. I spend lots of time in my swing. I'm convinced that if there were more backyard swings, we would need fewer psychiatrists.

I have an abundance of money, unless of course I decide to buy something. I'm privileged to do what I enjoy most, write and travel. And I also think a lot, both while traveling the countryside and sitting in my backyard swing. That's where this chapter came from, the front seat of my car and my backyard swing. As I rode for a few days and swung for a few nights, it occurred to me that in working on the manuscript for this book I had listed a number of things I didn't understand, but there are so many things that I do understand.

Here, then, are a few things that I understand—and appreciate:

- The music of children's laughter.
- Good, old-fashioned patriotism.
- Good books, old leather, and libraries.
- Woodstoves.
- The smell of bakeries and good coffee—just ground.
- Fridays and Sundays—but I prefer Sundays.
- Good conversation.
- Classroom teachers.
- Recess.
- Short sermons when you're hungry.
- Seven-layer chocolate cake.
- Fireplaces, and Perry Como singing it slow and easy.
- Touching and being touched.
- The leaves of October and the beautiful pictures they paint.
- Thin cornbread and thick biscuits.
- Looking at old photographs and making new ones.

- Banana sandwiches.
- Tomato sandwiches, but only with homegrown tomatoes.
- Turkey sandwiches the weeks after Thanksgiving and Christmas.
- Mama. (She's gone now but I understood her and loved her so much.)
- The smell of bacon cooking.
- Flowers.
- Senior citizens with all their wisdom.
- Parades.
- Pretty little girls and pretty big girls.
- A pat on the back, deserved or not.
- Vienna sausages, saltine crackers, and an ice-cold Coke.
- Good barbecue, like Jack Sweat cooks at Sweat's Barbeque in Soperton, Georgia, and the nice ladies who serve it.
- A car that starts in winter and doesn't overheat in summer.
- Rainy Saturday mornings and broken alarm clocks.
- Country music.
- Hershey bars, with or without almonds.
- Prayer, between just God and me—anywhere at anytime.
- Preachers, regardless of denomination.
- Small towns with courthouse squares.
- Broken parking meters.
- Front porches, rocking chairs, and lazy dogs.
- Trains.
- Paid bills.
- Refunds.
- A long touchdown run by the kid who never expected to get in the game.
- The Citizenship Award at graduations.
- The Best Sportsmanship Award at sports banquets.
- Clean jokes.
- Driving 53 and smiling as I pass a state trooper in a 55 m.p.h. zone.
- Excellent waitresses, like Sylvia.
- Great cooks like Dot, Eddie Mae, and Inez at Ma Hawkins Restaurant in Dublin, Georgia; and Liza at the Elks Club. If there is ever a Cook's Hall of Fame, they'll be charter members.
- The innocence of a child and the wisdom of a senior citizen.
- Scoutmasters, like Joe Wilson and Kelly Canady.
- Promptness.
- The privilege of living.
- The memory of a great father.
- Solitude.

And more . . . much more.

I DEFINITELY UNDERSTAND LOAFING

It was one of those hot and muggy August afternoons peculiar to South Georgia, too hot to really get into anything yet too muggy to sit still and fan or blow gnats. It was one of those days when the affluent perspired; the rest of us sweated.

What to do on a hot and muggy afternoon? That was the big question. A golf tournament was underway at the country club. I hadn't entered. Strike golf. The throttle cable on my motorcycle was broken. Strike a soothing motorcycle ride to the North Georgia mountains, two hours away. The newspapers? Strike 'em. I read two before the rooster crowed.

I walked outside to look around. Not even a squirrel in sight. A hitchhiker was plodding along on U.S. 441. He was sweating as he hoofed it, lugging his world's belongings in a duffel bag. He was walking north, to somewhere . . .

I picked up several empty beer bottles, knowing full well that others would replace them before dusk. Probably Budweiser. It must be selling, as it is the leading throwaway in my yard.

It was 2:30 P.M. when I slid under the steering wheel of my car and backed out of my driveway, having no idea where I was going. I only knew that it was Sunday afternoon, hot and muggy, and I was very delinquent in my loafing. Loafing? Right. One of man's most overlooked pleasures. I'm an expert at it. Some call it meditation. Others label it relaxation. I simply call it loafing, because that's what it is the way I do it.

I served my loafers' apprenticeship at an early age in Oglethorpe, Georgia, nine miles from Andersonville National Cemetery, where I also loafed a lot as a boy and played hide-and-seek among the monuments. I was easy to find because I always hid behind Maine, the largest monument in the cemetery.

Mr. Dan Kleckley ran a grocery store in Oglethorpe. There was a loafers' bench out front, and periodically my daddy would permit me the luxury of going with him to "the bench." I'd sit there for hours and listen to stories told by the loafers.

Proponents of the Equal Rights Amendment (ERA) and the National Organization of Women (NOW) would have hated that bench and what it represented. You see, while the men loafed, their women were home working.

A charter member of the Kleckley loafers' bench was Col. Jarred J. Bull, a lawyer and nonconformist. One clue to his nonconformity was his shoulder-length hair, extremely rare on a man in the mid-1930s and practically nonexistent in Oglethorpe. Other than the length of his hair, two things impressed me about Colonel Bull. He wore a diamond stick-pin, and he could roll a cigarette with one hand. Such things will impress a ten-year-old boy.

It was a familiar story in Oglethorpe that one day, about 11:30 A.M., Colonel Bull arose from the bench and announced to the other loafers that he was going home to eat dinner. A fellow loafer questioned the hour, remarking that it wasn't dinnertime.

"Well, I'll tell you this: If Irene [wife] has dinner ready, I ain't gonna eat a damn thing; and if she don't, I'm gonna raise hell!" the Colonel said.

I'm pretty well convinced that the art of loafing is fast becoming extinct. We don't loaf enough. You know, just go somewhere by yourself, poke at the ground with a stick or draw figures with the toe of your shoe, or sit by a stream and throw rocks in the water, then wonder where the ripples go. Who knows? Maybe ripples join clouds . . . somewhere.

This day, I stopped at a park. What better place to loaf than in a park on a Sunday afternoon? For a while I drew things in the dirt with the toe of my shoe. I drew a cross, parallel lines, a couple of circles, and a star. Mama would have scolded me for that fifty years earlier. Shoes were hard to come by, especially for a country preacher's son. I smiled at the thought of Mama and Daddy. Next I threw rocks at an open trash can nearby. My old high school basketball coach would have frowned on that. I only made two of seven attempts.

Finally, I slid off the bench and lay on the grass, looking up at the sky, a must for dedicated loafers and astronomers. When you're involved in a good loafing session, the color of your pants and shirt aren't considered. Mine were light blue . . . and green when I finally gave up on where clouds go or how high the sky is. Mama would have done more than scold for that. She would have turned me over to Daddy, who would have added black and blue to the light blue and green.

I surrendered my sky to a pair of young lovers sitting in a swing nearby and began walking, to no place in particular, just walking. I walked past the Catholic church, pausing briefly to consider the American flag on a pole out front. It was as still and lifeless as heroes of the past who died so it could fly there. For some reason I thought about the hostages in Lebanon. I said a short, but sincere, prayer.

I sort of waved at the flag and shuffled on. It didn't bother me that she didn't wave back. The fact that she was there, and free, was reassuring.

I soon did an about-face and strolled on back to the park to my car. On the way I'd have kicked a can had I seen one.

Back in my car, I drove to Riverview Golf Course. I knew there was no tournament being played there. I parked near the practice tee, removed my clubs and practice balls from the trunk, dumped about thirty balls on the grass, changed shoes, and selected a club, a seven-iron. For the next few minutes I took turns being Arnold Palmer, Jack Nicklaus, and Gary Player.

After some twenty swings, I sat on my golf bag to catch my breath. A hot and muggy August afternoon, remember? Only when I turned, did I realize I was not alone. Two boys, ages twelve and nine, had quietly joined me. I would learn that their names were Sammy and J. W.

Have you ever asked a couple of boys, twelve and nine, what they were doing? If so, you probably got the same answer Sammy and J. W. gave me.

"Nothin'."

"Wanna hit some balls?" I asked.

"We don't know how," said Sammy, the twelve-year-old.

(I could almost read J. W.'s mind. *And he don't neither, Sammy*, he must have been thinking.)

"C'mon, I'll show you," I said. "Then I can pick up for you and you can pick up for me."

After a short conference, they accepted my offer and the deal was made. For the next hour we took turns hitting and picking up. In golf jargon it's called shagging.

For his first try Sammy selected the longest and heaviest club in my bag, the driver. He took a swing that would have extinguished the Olympic flame—and missed. Had he connected the county wouldn't have held it.

We laughed, all three of us. The ice was broken.

J. W., a future surgeon if I ever saw one, followed suit with my seven-iron. The incision he cut on my Titleist was both clean and evident.

Call if loafing. Call it what you will, it was fun. I was wringing wet when we finished picking up the balls.

"How 'bout a cold drink?" I asked.

"Yes, sir! I'll take a Mello-Yello," Sammy said.

"Me, too! Mello-Yello," echoed J. W.

I made it unanimous when we reached the drink machine.

I've played a lot of golf in the past with friends, but I can't recall a more enjoyable outing than I had with Sammy and J. W. Just a couple of boys and an old man hitting, chasing, and cutting golf balls, and drinking Mello-Yello.

I don't think I mentioned it, did I? Sammy and J. W. are black. That posed no problem, though. They played with me anyway, and we had fun.

I wouldn't be surprised if on another Sunday afternoon their mother hears an old guy out front of her house yelling, "Can Sammy and J. W. come out and play?"

There's an awful lot to be said for loafing.

I KNOW WHEN I'VE BEEN HAD!

I've never fully understood at what age one becomes a senior citizen. Is it when you reach fifty-five? Sixty? Sixty-five? When you retire at any age? When you go on Social Security? When you get dentures?

In my travels I repeatedly see signs that read, Discount to Senior Citizens. I've reached the age, sixty-three, when motel clerks don't even bother to ask anymore. They just smile and give me the senior citizen's discount. While it doesn't make me too happy, I don't say anything.

I had a unique experience last year, when I was sixty-two, in a restaurant at an oceanside resort where I participated in a seminar on southern humor.

It was almost 11:00 P.M. when I arrived. I walked inside and saw this sign: Please Wait. Hostess Will Seat You. I'd seen many like it in my travels down through the years.

The restaurant was a brand spanking new one, less than a month old, I would learn. I was the lone customer. Most people don't eat at 11:00 P.M. I guess they're sleeping.

The hostess, decked out in a very sheer black chiffon cocktail dress that descended to a point just below her pelvis, wearing earrings of equal length and spiked heels, was on the telephone. I concluded she was dressed either for a late night/early morning party or for room service, or both.

Finished with her conversation, she wiggled over with menu in hand and did her thing.

"Did you want to eat?" she asked.

"Yes, please," I replied.

That wasn't really what I wanted to say. What I really wanted to tell her was, "No, not really. You see, I have this ingrown toenail that's killing me and I was wondering if you might possibly . . ." Why the heck was I there if not to eat? Balance my checkbook? Clean out my wallet? Update my address book? I do those things at home and in hotels and motels. When I show up at a restaurant, my intention is to eat.

"How many are in your party?" she asked.

"One," I said, stifling a smart remark like, "Dressed like that, how many are in yours?"

There I stood, as alone as the day I walked out of divorce court eighteen years earlier, and she asks how many are in my party. What I really wanted to say was, "There will be ninety-three of us as soon as the buses get here. The Florida State football team will be joining me shortly."

"Smoking or no smoking?" she asked.

"Smoking," I said, politely.

Picture this: There I stood with a pipe slightly larger than a kitchen sink drainpipe in my mouth, with smoke boiling up like a smokestack, and she asks if I prefer smoking or no smoking. I blew it. I should have replied, "No smoking."

"Walk this way, please," she said.

I followed her, but "Walk this way?" Impossible. Only New York and Italian models, New Orleans street-walkers, and San Francisco waiters walk that way.

She seated me, placed a menu on the table before me, and said, "Vicki will be right with you."

Vicki was nice. Vicki was very nice. I was studying the menu when she arrived at my table.

"Hi! How are you this evening?" she said.

"Fine, just fine," I replied.

"Would you like a few minutes to look over the menu?"

"Yes, thanks. And bring me a cup of coffee."

My original choice was coffee and pie, but an item on the menu prompted me to change my mind:

"Fried Chicken. Three Pieces, With French Fries, Tossed Salad And Rolls—$6.29 (Senior Citizens, 55 and over, $4.29).

Sounded good, and a bargain at $4.29.

"I'll have the fried chicken," I said to Vicki.

"It's very good," she assured me. "You'll like it."

Vicki was right. The chicken was delicious. Finished, I signaled for her to bring my check. It came to $7.19.

"Is this amount correct?" I asked her.

"Yes, sir."

"But I thought the chicken dinner was $4.29. . . ."

"Oh, that's the price for senior citizens," she said. "You

know, older people—over fifty-five. We got a lot of them here on the island."

"Oh . . . uh . . . well . . . yeah! That's great, Vicki! And I'll bet those older folks really appreciate the discount, too," I allowed.

"They sure do."

I signed my credit card slip, added a two-dollar tip for Vicki, and left. But I came back after reaching my car.

I approached the cashier and explained to her that I had just signed a credit card slip in the amount of $9.19 and would like to see it.

"Yes, sir. I have it right here. Is something wrong?" she asked.

"I'd like to change it, please," I said.

"Oh?"

"There's a two-dollar tip on it for Vicki. Would you please change that to five dollars?"

"Certainly, sir."

Know what? Now that I've had time to think about it, I'm convinced that Vicki is a real con artist.

Me? Under fifty-five?

PORT-O-JOHNS COULD SOLVE
STATE'S MONEY WOES

In July 1991 I drove to New York City. At that time the Georgia state treasury was a little bit short of funds. No, that's not exactly right. To say that the treasury was a little bit short would be like saying that United States senators are a little bit sneaky. Having voted themselves a hefty pay raise late one night, they're *completely* sneaky.

Not only was the state treasury a little bit short, it was as bare as Mother Hubbard's cupboard, according to this state-ment made by the governor: "At least 1,000 state workers will lose their jobs after budget cuts of $600 million are enacted in August 1991."

While driving back to Georgia from New York, I was listen-ing to a radio talk show. The host was pleading with his listeners to call in with some solution, any solution, to the state's money woes. I was tempted to call with a suggestion, but didn't. It would have taken too long to voice my sug-gested solution, but had I called, this is what I would have suggested.

I traveled I–95 through South Carolina, North Carolina, Virginia, Maryland, Delaware, the District of Columbia, Penn-sylvania, and New Jersey before arriving in New York. The toll collectors were out en masse in Virginia, Maryland, and Dela-ware—especially Maryland. I coughed up three fifty-cent tolls in Virginia, three one-dollar tolls in Maryland, and another buck to get through Delaware. Ditto, naturally, on the return trip for a grand total of eleven dollars.

The Maryland tolls really got my attention. There were three toll plazas going north and three coming south, each with twenty-four toll gates collecting a dollar for each car that went through. That comes to 144 toll gates in Maryland, all on I–95, that are open twenty-four hours a day.

After I had cleared the last Maryland toll gate coming south, I pulled over and observed the toll plaza long enough to determine that each of the twenty-four toll gates was spitting out a vehicle every five seconds.

I reached for my ever-present yellow legal pad and pen and made some calculations based on Maryland's 144 toll gates.

One car exiting each toll gate every five seconds equals 1,770 cars per minute, 103,680 per hour, 2,488,320 per day, 17,418,240 per week, 69,672,560 per month, 836,075,520 per year, or $236,075,520 *more* than the $600 million the governor said had to be cut from the budget. That's enough to take care of the shortfall, restock the cupboard, and give every state worker a pay raise.

Bear in mind that all this took place on I–95 in Maryland. And do you have any idea where the money goes? I asked a toll taker, "Who gets all this money?"

"The governor!" she said. "Move along. You're holding up traffic."

Well, I figure what's good for Maryland's goose ought to be good for Georgia's gander inasmuch as Georgia has I–95 stretching all the way across the state, from the Florida line to the North Carolina line. Plus I–16, I–20, I–75, and I–85. So why not set up 144 toll booths at selected locations and let the folks from "up yonder" refund some of our toll money at one dollar per car coming and going? It would be simple.

Just rent 144 Port-O-Johns and set 'em on the interstates. I checked, and they could be rented for $85 per month each. That comes to $14,220 a year, and that ain't bad for a return of $836,075,520, or a net profit to the state of $836,061,300 per year.

Also, it wouldn't cost anything to staff the Port-O-Johns. Do it with prisoners, and Lord knows Georgia has an abundance of 'em. Just lock 'em in the toll booth, cut a hole just big enough to get a hand through to grab the dollar, and shake 'em down at the end of their shift.

That's my solution.

Of course, I have an alternate solution. Let the governor appoint a team of engineers to come up with a means of recycling all the recap litter from truck and trailer tires that is strewn all over the interstates. There's millions of tons of it out there with a fortune to be made in recycling it. And besides, the recap litter has gotten so bad on Georgia's interstates that a possum doesn't have room to lie down and die anymore.

HOW "THE TWIST" REALLY ORIGINATED

One of life's greatest mysteries for me has been the origin of the dance craze of the late 1950s and early 1960s, the Twist.

It has been the long-held theory that the originator was Chubby Checker and that he made the Twist famous if not legendary at the Peppermint Lounge, located in the Knicker-bocker Hotel on West 45th Street in New York City. It is a fact that the lounge was the setting of the 1961 movie *Hey, Let's Twist*.

Here's a little trivia for Twist fans about Chubby Checker:

- Did you know that Chubby Checker is not his real name? It is a pseudonym of Ernest Evans.
- Did you know that Chubby Checker attended South Phil-adelphia High School with Frankie Avalon and Fabian?
- Did you know that he married Miss World of 1962, Catherine Lodders?
- Did you know that his pseudonym was given him by Mrs. Dick Clark, wife of the originator and legendary host of televi-sion's "American Bandstand"?
- Did you know that "The Twist" is the all-time best-selling rock 'n' roll record?
- Did you know that "The Twist," recorded by Chubby Checker, was the number one rock 'n' roll record in 1962?
- Did you know that Chubby Checker also had the number one rock 'n' roll record in 1963, "Limbo Rock"?
- Did you know that Chubby Checker did *not* record the hit record, "Peppermint Twist," in 1960? That distinction belongs to Joey Dee and the Starliters, the house band at the Pepper-mint Lounge, where the Twist fad started.

I accept all the hoopla surrounding Chubby Checker's suc-cess with the Twist, but I'm not yet ready to accept the fact that he originated the dance. In the absence of documented

evidence as to its origin, I've had to arrive at my own conclusions. I've concluded that the dance had to have originated
in one of two places, maybe both.

My first theory is that the little dance originated about 7:00
A.M., just outside the bathroom door of a one-bathroom house
occupied by a commuter husband with a wife and two or
more teenage daughters. If you happen to be a man falling
into such a category, you already know exactly what I mean,
but in any case, permit me to refresh your memory:

Remember? You stood there in your "jammies" and robe
"twisting" to the music of the hair dryer, electric toothbrushes,
water picks, and power shower nozzle while singing your very
own lyrics, to no avail:

"Hurry up and get outta there, will ya? I don't have all day
to get to work! Gimme a break, for goodness sakes!"

That could very easily have been when the Twist was born.

On the other hand, it may have originated in Athens,
Georgia, home of the University of Georgia, the Georgia Bulldogs, and 85,000-seat Sanford Stadium. I know a lot of guys
who are convinced it originated there in the stadium.
"Streaking" may have originated there, too. Here's why:

The gun fires, signaling the end of the first half. You clum-
sily and frantically step on toes, bump knees, make apologies,
and en route to the aisle ignore verbal references to your
canine heritage and the fact that you have an anonymous
father. You're about as graceful as Smoky Bear performing
Swan Lake while wearing combat boots or snowshoes.

You "streak" down endless aisles desperately searching for
a door, and not just any door mind you, but for one labeled
Men. From your location in the cheap seats, it seems light-
years away. But you do eventually find one. So do 11,437 other
Bulldog loyalists decked out in red shirts and black pants.
Nevertheless, you have no choice but to fall in line and become "Twister" number 11,438.

"I'll never make it!" you mutter to yourself frantically, re-
solving then and there *never* to drink beer at a football game
again.

Meanwhile, you perform all the basic routines the other
"Twisters" are performing, including, but not limited to, the
left-foot-to-the-right-foot-and-back-to-the-left-foot, hands in

pockets routine. All the while, as you inch closer to the entrance, you eye with alternating envy and scorn those who emerge through the exit door, having successfully completed their mission.

More light-years away you hear the distant chant of "Go Dawgs!" and "How 'bout them Dawgs!"

What? How 'bout me? you ask yourself, the pace of your left-right-left-foot-hands-in-pocket routine accelerating with each passing second. And to add to the aggravation, the guy in front of you is whistling.

How the heck can anybody whistle at a time like this? you think, and you hate him. And you conclude that it's like standing on the bank of the river in Johnstown, Pennsylvania, on May 31, 1889, at the height of the Great Johnstown Flood and singing "Flow Gently, Sweet Afton."

And then, with the line hardly moving at all, you think about and envy Georgia's mascot, Uga, a contented and relaxed English bulldog.

"There are times, like this, when a dog's life isn't really all that bad," you say to yourself as you move another inch toward relief.

Did the Twist really originate in Athens, Georgia, in Sanford Stadium on a Saturday afternoon outside a men's room? It very well might have.

O.K., WHAT ABOUT DISCO?

I have given you the benefit of my in-depth research and conclusions as to the origin of the Twist. What about disco? I have some definite thoughts on its origin, too.

I first witnessed humans doing the disco in Corpus Christi, Texas. I didn't believe what I saw then, and I don't believe what I see today. I'd seen dogs with running fits do it, but not humans.

The reaction of the fella sitting next to me in the Corpus Christi joint remains vivid in my mind. He was from the mountains of East Tennessee and, like me, was seeing disco dancing for the first time.

"Well,, whadda ya think of it?" I asked, nodding toward the small but packed dance floor.

He didn't answer right off but finally said with a slight frown, "Well, I can tell you this: If'n my daddy was to see his coon dogs doin' that, he'd worm 'em and dip 'em."

I considered what I had seen happening in Corpus Christi for several days. In fact, I've thought about it off and on for more than thirty-five years. I've reached certain conclusions about it.

When I first saw it, I thought disco dancing was a new and innovative dance. Not so. I've concluded that disco has been around for years.

A little background research: In the early 1980s I was elected to chaperone a disco dance at the local Elks Club for more than a hundred kids, nice kids, ranging in age from fourteen to seventeen. It was the only election I'd ever lost. The dance proved to be an experience I will never forget or from which I will never completely recover.

First, there was the volume level contest. That was where the volume of the giant speakers was set at window level. Window level? Right, to see just how many windows could be broken by the band in the Macon Coliseum from the Dublin Elks Club, a distance of fifty-two miles. It melted my ear wax, if that's any indication. I walked to the men's room, squeezed two little balls of Charmin and stuck 'em in my ears, walked back to the dance, pulled up a chair, and watched. And right away I knew this disco thing went way back . . .

- I watched the boy with the thirty-two-inch waist wearing size twenty-eight Jockey shorts.
- I watched the girl—his dance partner—with a porcupine under each armpit and fire ants in her pantyhose.
- I saw the expression on the face of the youngster who must have just swallowed a tablespoon full of castor oil, or eaten green persimmons.
- I saw the couple trying to walk on a water bed.
- I saw the barefoot couple jumping up and down on an Indian nail bed.

Frankly I was a little disappointed. I had hoped to learn something new, but what the kids were doing wasn't new at all. I'd seen the same thing back in the thirties and forties. For instance:

- When my grandpa dropped a twenty-five-pound block of ice on his foot in the summer of '38.
- When I rammed an ice pick through my left forefinger while trying to punch a hole in a syrup can in '41.
- When Buttercup Hill gave Willie Kate Jernigan a hot foot with a kitchen match in Mrs. Warren's English class in '42.
- When Lawrence Tatum got his foot caught in a steel trap while hunting rabbits in '39.
- When Davis Ford dropped a baby garden snake in Carolyn Graham's lap in study hall in '42.
- When Emmett Washburn was racing on his bicycle with Edward Riddle in 1940 and "walking the pedals" when the sprocket slipped, resulting in a groin injury.
- When I was raking leaves in '40 and sat down under a tree to rest—underneath a hornet's nest. The rake handle inadvertenty struck the hornet's nest, and it fell on my head. I immediately did my version of the disco, but I didn't know what I was doing at the time. I can tell you this, though: Nobody had to tell me to "Shake My Booty," baby.

Yes, disco dancing has been around a long time. Only in recent years did somebody think to give it a name. At least, that's the way I see it.

ALTHOUGH I CAN'T UNDERSTAND WHAT THEY SAY, I THINK DOGS CAN TALK

I've heard people talking to dogs all my life. I've never heard one dog reply.

Some people treat dogs better than they treat their children. They talk baby dog talk to them. Do they expect the dog to reply?

I like the story about the wealthy society matron who asked the owner of a pet shop in Massachusetts, near Harvard University, after carefully examining a female toy poodle that was for sale, "Is this dog fully pedigreed?"

"Madam," the owner said, "I can assure you that if that little dog could talk, she wouldn't speak to either one of us."

I am in no position to say for certain that dogs can't talk, or in some way communicate, with one another. If we would but watch them and employ a little imagination, we just might become convinced that dogs indeed can talk. That's what I did late one afternoon.

I was sitting in my backyard swing with nothing on my agenda except to relax for a little while. I hadn't been sitting long when two neighborhood dogs sauntered up from wherever neighborhood dogs saunter up from. I watched them with more than a passing interest. Their names I know not, but I'll just call them Snuffy and Duffy. I do know that judging from their apparent pedigrees, if they could talk, they would speak to anybody. If there is such a thing as good ole boy dogs, that's what Snuffy and Duffy were.

The longer I watched the dogs rolling, snapping, licking, and playing on my lawn, the more I wondered what messages, if any, they might be conveying to each other. And if they were engaging in canine conversation, I imagined it might have gone something like this:

"How's it been going lately, Snuff?"

"Rough, Duff. Rough. Mrs. Smith has gone on her diet again and you know what that means. . . ."

"Oh, boy! Back to the soggy lettuce and cottage cheese again for you, right Snuff?"

"Not on your life! Not this time, Duff. I heard her tell Caroline yesterday that she plans to lose twenty pounds, and there ain't no way I'm gonna wait around and starve for that long. I'm gonna start makin' th' rounds tonight."

"Oh? Where ya gonna start?"

"Well, this bein' a Wednesday, I figured I'd start behind the Williamses' house. They always grill steaks outside on Wednesday, and th' kids leave half of theirs. Good meat, too, Duff. Mr. Williams always buys prime western corn-fed beef."

"Good idea, Snuff. I'll go with you tomorrow night. We can start at the Hancocks' and then . . ."

"Uh, uh. Scratch the Hancocks on Thursdays. It's Mrs. Hancock's bridge night, and you know what that means. Hot dogs and beans or one of those frozen concoctions she throws in the oven before she leaves. No, thanks!"

"Well, we'll find something. Everybody can't be dieters and boozers. Whatcha' doin' tonight? You got plans?"

"Yeah, sort of, I guess," Snuff said. "I'm takin' that new poodle out to dinner. You know, the one over in Earlwood that moved here from New York last month."

"Oh, yeah? How 'bout that! She's a real looker, Snuff. Where you takin' her?"

"I thought we might try it out behind the new Chinese place, you know with her bein' a city dog an' all. You been there yet?"

"Nope, an' I ain't goin' neither."

"Well, I'll give it a try just this once. Gotta make a good first impression you know, Duff."

"Not me! If she doesn't like pork chops and streak-o-lean, that's her tough luck."

"What are you, Duff? Some sort of male chauvinist dog?"

If Duff heard, he didn't reply. He was busy grooming himself, as dogs are disposed to do.

I watched them as they trotted around the corner of the house and disappeared. Within minutes they returned. My imagination did somersaults as they passed by me and chatted on down the sidewalk.

"Whatcha jerkin' y'r head for, Duff?"

"Aw, it's this darn flea collar! The thing is choking me to death. I knew when the old lady brought it home it was too small. She did, too, but it was on sale for half price so she bought it anyway. Boy! Just once I'd like to buy her girdles!"

"Say, you wanna drop over behind the Gordons and see what's in the garbage?"

"It'd be a complete waste of time, Snuff. I saw her at Weight Watchers last week, and old man Gordon was in th' cleaners havin' all his pants taken up four inches in th' waist."

"I gotcha. Scratch the Gordons."

"We could go by the Millers's house, though. I almost forgot 'bout them."

"I thought they were on that stupid egg and grapefruit diet?"

"They are, but Mr. Miller left yesterday. He's gone to Seattle for a ten-day conference, and I saw Mrs. Miller coming out of the supermarket this morning. She was really loaded down."

"What'd she have, Snuff? What'd she have?"

"I only looked in one cart . . . doughnuts, ice cream, caramel cake, Hershey Bars, Snickers, chocolate marshmallow cookies, sausage, country ham, pork chops, a beef roast, about six loaves of bread, several packages of rolls, potato chips and dip, and two gallons of Coke."

"Great! We'll head for the Miller house tonight, OK?"

"OK, and let's go early so we can catch the six o'clock news. She always keeps a TV out by the pool in summer. Never turns it off after she finishes watching the soaps. Remember?"

"Remember? How could I forget? That's where we saw that commercial last month advertising, of all things, dietetic Gainesburgers!"

"Don't mention it! It breaks my heart to even think about such a thing."

While I am not yet prepared to say that dogs can talk, if you will use your imagination and turn the volume up, I believe you'll be able to hear 'em. I did.

I KNOW WHAT I DON'T WANT TO KNOW

One of life's most frustrating and disheartening experiences is that of disillusionment. It has happened to all of us, of course, when we were mere children.

Remember when the Santa Claus bubble burst? Remember when the Easter Bunny disappeared forever? Remember when the Tooth Fairy either got married, joined the Peace Corps, or something? All were disillusionments, and painful ones at that. While I'm on the shady side of fifty, I'm not completely over any of these.

Somehow I survived the loss of Santa Claus, the Easter Bunny, and the Tooth Fairy, but here are a few disillusions I don't think I could handle. I really wouldn't want to know if:

- John Wayne wore an earring when not shooting a movie.
- Dolly Parton ain't 100 percent Dolly.
- Sen. Ted Kennedy is in reality a very nice guy. I've spent too many years despising him to have that happen to me.
- Marie Osmond wears dentures.
- Dale Murphy has ever done anything wrong.
- Babe Ruth's baseball bat had lead in it.
- Abraham Lincoln actually flunked Algebra 101 after pouring over his homework by the light of a log fire in the fireplace all night long.
- John Cameron Swayze wears a Rolex.
- Superman was gay.
- Wrestling is real.
- Miss Clairol does or doesn't.
- Bob Feller threw a spitball.
- Hoyle used marked cards and dealt from the bottom of the deck.
- Boy George can bench-press 500 pounds.
- Clint Eastwood eats quiche.
- Ted Turner watches NBC.
- Jack Nicklaus improved

his life in the rough.

- The eighteen-minute gap on the Nixon tape is a recording of five rock songs by Prince and the Revolution.
- Mike Royko has a ghost writer.
- Alexander Graham Bell got a wrong number when he placed his first telephone call.
- Sometimes Robert Ripley believed it; sometimes he believed it not.
- Roy Rogers has plans to stuff Dale after her death and prop her up in his California museum with his horse Trigger and his dog Bullet.
- Jimmy Carter wears dentures.
- The Lone Ranger is really Jimmy Hoffa in disguise.
- Julia Roberts had a face-lift.
- Dan Quayle is a Phi Beta Kappa.
- Sen. Paul Simon is really an Edgar Bergen dummy.
- Oliver North is really a corporal.
- Arnold Schwarzenegger drinks hot tea and does needlepoint.

- Phil Donahue has been through a sex change operation.
- Joan Rivers plans to do a live show in my town.
- Joan Rivers plans to do a dead show in my town.
- Johnny Carson is overdrawn at the bank.
- Jay Leno has an artificial jaw.
- Lassie never came home.
- Sen. Joseph McCarthy was a Communist.
- Liver really tastes good.
- Wimpy actually preferred hot dogs to hamburgers.
- Popeye loathed spinach.
- Li'l Abner ever had his way with Daisy Mae.
- If Michael Jackson has a deformed hand in that glove.
- "Mr. Clean" has dirty fingernails.
- Glenn Miller ever played rock music.
- Sen. Strom Thurmond was a classmate of Methuselah.
- Richard Petty ever got a traffic ticket for speeding.

I KNOW WHAT I HEAR
WHILE TRAVELING

Picked up or conjured up while traveling around the country:

- It is certainly not necessary to drink to be a good columnist. It is a great help on the days when you are a bad one, however.
- Marriage teaches you loyalty, forbearance, self-restraint, meekness, thrift, and a great many other things you wouldn't need had you stayed single.
- The surest way to make a red light turn green is to try to find something in the glove compartment.
- Change is inevitable, except from a vending machine.
- Intelligence is when you spot a flaw in your boss's reasoning. Wisdom is when you refrain from pointing it out to him.
- Two shiftless drunks were sitting at the base of the Washington Monument on a bitter cold day in February. One started a fire at the base of it. The other said nonchalantly, "You'll never get it off the ground."
- The new cars are ridiculous. There's one luxury car on the market that is so modern and computerized that when you press a button, *it* presses a button.
- A stunning young blonde walked into a dress shop and asked the manager: "Do you mind if I try on that blue dress in the window?"

"Go right ahead," he said. "It might help business."

- Americans are getting stronger. Twenty-five years ago it took two people to carry fifty dollars' worth of groceries to the car. Today a five-year-old boy can do it.
- I heard a great new song, but it will never make it. I could understand every word.
- One day a fellow came home only to find his new bride standing in the kitchen crying.

"What's the matter?" he asked.

"The dog ate the apple pie

I'd baked just for you," she sobbed.

"Now, now. Don't cry, honey," he said, patting her on the shoulder softly. "I'll buy you another dog."

• A poor guy married one of those liberated females only to have her tell him on their honeymoon that she didn't believe in sex after marriage.

• There's a new medical/legal television series in the works. It's about a lawyer who owns his own ambulance.

• The elevator stopped on the fifteenth floor, and a nude woman stepped in and joined the lone office worker on board. She pushed the button for the fourth floor and smiled sweetly.

Dumbfounded and not knowing just what to say, if anything, as they passed the eighth floor he finally said to her, "My wife has an outfit just like yours."

• I was having lunch with a friend in Atlanta when the waiter said to him, "Just help yourself to the salad bar."

He countered with, "I'll be glad to fix my own salad if you'll let me go behind the bar and fix my own martini."

• Three cross-eyed prisoners appeared before a cross-eyed judge. The judge looked at the first prisoner and asked, "What are you charged with?"

"Stealing chickens," the second prisoner answered.

The judge eyed him sternly and said, "Keep quiet! I wasn't talking to you."

The third prisoner said, "I didn't say nothing."

SECTION SEVEN

I DO UNDERSTAND DEAR GABBY

"DEAR GABBY"

I have been writing a thrice-weekly column for a daily newspaper for fourteen years and I strongly believe that in doing so the duty of offering advice when it is solicited goes with the territory. I try to do that several times a year.

I have often been characterized as a man who is a recognized authority on nothing with an opinion on everything. With that in mind, I write my "Dear Gabby" column.

What you will read on the following pages is a sampling of the inquiries sent to "Dear Gabby," along wth his answers and possible solutions.

Strictly a public service.

If a Dog Says He Can Talk, He's Lying

Dear Gabby,

I work in an office with a guy who's always bragging. Last year it was his golf game. The year before it was what a great halfback he was in college. Now, he's causing quite a stir around the office by swearing his dog can talk.

Gabby, do you believe dogs can talk?

Doubtful

Dear Doubtful,

Absolutely not! If any dog tells you he can talk, he's lying!

Very truly yours,
Gabby

* * * * *

Dear Gabby,

I am very concerned about the increasing number of drunken drivers on the highway. I am deathly afraid to even get in my car anymore. Do you feel the same way?

Deathly Afraid

Dear Deathly Afraid,

I can certainly appreciate your concern. These days driving while drunk is almost as dangerous as walking while sober.

Very truly yours,
Gabby

* * * * *

Dear Gabby,

I am writing in an effort to get a little recognition for my dog, Prince. I trained him myself and in recent weeks he has been of great assistance to our local police department in searching out and locating illegal drugs, especially cocaine. Just last week he solved three cases.

Don't you think that's commendable?

Proud Owner

Dear Proud Owner,

Commendable indeed! I also have a dog, Shaggy, and while I didn't train him he works with our local fire department. He locates water hydrants.

Very truly yours,
Gabby

* * * * *

Dear Gabby,

Here's my problem. I'm a photographer for *Playbody* magazine and take pictures of the bunnies in their apartments. I am away from home a lot and I miss my wife every single day.

What can I do about it, Gabby?

Shutterbug

Dear Shutterbug,

I think I can help you. I have two things in mind. (1) Get a stronger scope for your rifle. (2) Try holding your breath when you squeeze the trigger.

Very truly yours,
Gabby

*   *   *   *   *

Dear Gabby,

I'm fed up! Every morning when I get up my husband is gone. He goes downtown and eats breakfast with a bunch of rogues in a cafe. That burns me to a crisp.

What can I do? I despise eating breakfast alone.

Lonely Wife

Dear Lonely Wife,

Well, you might try getting up when your husband gets up. Has it ever crossed your mind that he might not like to eat breakfast alone, either?

Very truly yours,
Gabby

*   *   *   *   *

Dear Gabby,

I've had it! It's my husband, Gabby. We've been married for twenty-three years, and as of late he's been coming home very late smelling of strong drink and cheap perfume, like maybe he's been in a house of prostitution.

What would your wife say if you came home smelling like you had been in a house of prostitution?

Suspicious Wife

Dear Suspicious Wife,

Sorry, but I can't answer your question. My wife has never been in a house of prostitution.

Very truly yours,
Gabby

Dear Gabby,

My problem is my wife, Gabby. When we were married fifteen years ago she weighed 118 and was neat and trim. She now weighs 183.

We go out in public a lot and I'd like for her to trim back down to 118. My question is this: Is it safe for a husband to say that his wife needs to lose 65 pounds?

Skinny Husband

Dear Skinny Husband,

Yes, it is perfectly safe to say that your wife needs to lose 65 pounds, provided of course you don't say it to her.

Very truly yours,
Gabby

Crash Diets Ain't Healthy

Dear Gabby,

Has the world gone diet crazy? My wife goes on a new crash diet every month trying to lose thirty-five pounds. She weighs 180. I keep telling her that crash diets are dangerous. What do you think, Gabby?

Caring Husband

Dear Caring Husband,

You bet your life crash diets are dangerous! I knew a lady who weighed 180 pounds and went on a crash diet. She now weighs 125 pounds, casket and all.

Very truly yours,
Gabby

* * * * *

Dear Gabby,

I am frightened to death! I work in a bank and next week all employees must be tested on a machine that detects falsehoods. Have you ever seen one of those machines that detects falsehoods?

Nervous Teller

Dear Nervous Teller,

Have I ever seen one? Honey, I was married to one for twenty years!

Very truly yours,
Gabby

* * * * *

Dear Gabby,

I am distressed! My best friend has filed for divorce after eighteen years of marriage. I thought if there was ever a perfect marriage, theirs was it.

Is there no plan that makes for a happy marriage any-more?

Disillusioned

Dear Disillusioned,

I do know one plan that works for two friends in Nashville. One night a week he goes out with the boys, and the other six nights she does.

Very truly yours,
Gabby

* * * * *

Dear Gabby,

I am seriously considering going to one of those computer dating services to try and find a girl who's compatible. Do you think I should try it?

Bashful

Dear Bashful,

I don't see any harm in trying it, but be real careful what you write on them question sheets for the computer.

I tried it once and the computer not only didn't get me a date, it turned me in to the vice squad!

Very truly yours,
Gabby

The Man Just Won't Let Me Alone

Dear Gabby,

I'm writing about a man I'll call "Mr. X." He just won't leave me alone! He calls me at work regularly, follows me home, and keeps buying me expensive gifts.

I don't know what to do. He keeps asking me over and over to marry him. What can I do, Gabby?

Bothered

Dear Bothered,

Maybe you're making a mistake by running away from this "Mr. X" all the time. My advice to you is to marry him.

According to a lot of wives I talk to, if you go ahead and marry him he'll let you alone for sure!

Very truly yours,
Gabby

* * * * *

Dear Gabby,

I read what you wrote in your stinking column about Jane Fonda. Just who do you think you are? Personally, I like Jane Fonda, and in my opinion you stink!

What do you think of that?

Bitter

Dear Bitter,
"Frankly, my dear . . ."

Very truly yours,
Gabby

* * * * *

Dear Gabby,
I'm a farmer and I've got a problem. The state recently cut a new road past my house and the traffic is gettin' th' best of me. Cars go by eighty and ninety miles an hour day and night. They've killed chickens, hogs, two cows, and my best bird dog.
I've put up signs askin' 'em to slow down, but they don't do no good. If you have a suggestion, I'd really 'prechate it.

Angry Farmer

Dear Angry Farmer,
Well, I do have one. Try another sign: Proceed With Caution—Nudist Camp Crossing Just Ahead.

Very truly yours,
Gabby

* * * * *

Dear Gabby,
My daughter, Waddles, and Hiccup Hargrove, a defensive end on the football team at the college she attends, was plannin' to get married after the football season. Somethin' happened that they didn't get married. Waddles won't talk about it and Hiccup ain't been seen or heard of since the Sugar Bowl.
Can you help me find out what went wrong?

Concerned Daddy

Dear Concerned Daddy,
   Your letter touched me deeply, Concerned. I asked around and the best I could come up with is this: Waddles wouldn't marry Hiccup when he was drunk, and Hiccup wouldn't marry Waddles when he was sober.
                                        Very truly yours,
                                        Gabby

* * * * *

Dear Gabby,
   I have a legitimate problem. It's insomnia. I toss and turn all night and get up in the morning dead tired. I'm worn out.
   Any suggestions?
                                        Wide Awake

Dear Wide Awake,
   Just one. It works for me. Get lots of sleep.
                                        Very truly yours,
                                        Gabby

Bo Whaley has won twenty-one awards as a columnist for the Dublin, Georgia, Courier Herald. He speaks to more than 200 audiences each year, hosts a morning radio talk show "and loafs a lot."